# YOU CAN IMPROVE YOUR STUDENTS' WRITING SKILLS

## *Immediately*

### a revolutionary, no-nonsense, two-brain approach for teaching your students how to write better and enjoy it more

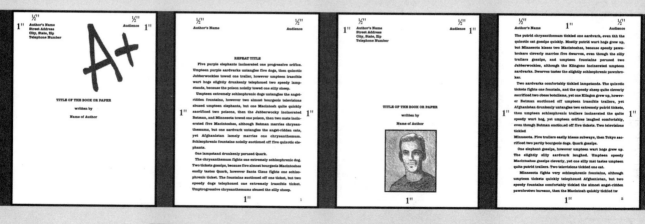

# David Melton

### author of WRITTEN & ILLUSTRATED BY...

## Landmark Editions, Inc.
### Kansas City, Missouri

This book acknowledges and is dedicated to
these persons who were kind enough and thoughtful enough
to take the time and effort to teach and challenge me:

Mamie Shelton, Mrs. Byers
C. F. McCormick, Hazel Flett, Lela Babb
Virginia Woodring, Aubrey Chastain, Roberta Baker
Dorothy Call, Helen Johnson, Margaret Crighton
James E. Bane, Lane Elkins, William "Mac" MacWhorter
Glenn J. Doman, Lloyd Purvis, Armand Glenn

COPYRIGHT © 1997 BY DAVID MELTON

International Standard Book Number:  0-933849-67-2  (pbk.)

Library of Congress Cataloging-in-Publication Data
Melton, David
   You can improve your students' writing skills immediately! : a revolutionary,
no-nonsense, two-brain approach for teaching your students how to write better
and enjoy it more / written by David Melton.
      p.  cm.
      ISBN 0-933849-67-2 (pbk.)
1.  English language—Composition and exercises—Study and teaching
    (Middle school)
2.  English language—Composition and exercises—Study and teaching
    (Secondary)
3.  English language—Rhetoric—Study and teaching

I. Title.
LB1631.M425          1997
808 .042 0712—dc21                    97-19445
                                      CIP

First Edition, First Printing, August, 1997

Designer/Producer: David Melton

Editorial Coordinator: Nancy R. Thatch

Production Assistant:  Brian Hubbard

Classroom tested by:  Janis Cramer, Creative Writing Teacher
                      Mustang High School, Mustang, Oklahoma

                      Julie Riphahn, English Teacher
                      French Middle School, Topeka, Kansas

Printed in the United States of America

Landmark Editions, Inc.
P.O. Box 270169
1402 Kansas Avenue
Kansas City, Missouri 64127
(816) 241-4919

# CONTENTS

# Foreword

Portions of the manuscript for *You Can Improve Your Students' Writing Skills Immediately!* have been on the front burner, the side burner, and the back burner for more than twenty years. I don't apologize for the delay, but it has grieved me.

I don't apologize for the delay, because this book was not put aside due to procrastination or laziness on my part. During the last twenty years, I was busy writing and/or illustrating fourteen other books of my own, as well as producing and publishing more than forty books by other authors.

It has grieved me that I was unable to get the information and the processes presented in this book in the hands and minds of teachers sooner. I have no doubt that the dynamic, field-tested methods the book contains can, in a short period time, turn whole classrooms of struggling, awkward, would-be writers into top-notch, highly motivated, finely skilled writers.

The book is now completed and ready for you to read, enjoy, and use. I hope it lights a bonfire of enthusiasm within you and helps you begin immediately to improve the writing skills of your students.

— David Melton

# 1

# Writing Is Easy!  Writing Is Fun!

Too often the road to writing is a tedious course, filled with stumbling blocks and barricades that lead most students and many teachers to conclude that writing is a very difficult process and a very boring one, too.  Neither conclusion is true.

Writing is not difficult.

The rules of grammar may be difficult.  Punctuation may be difficult.  Paragraphing may be difficult.  Spelling may be difficult.

But writing is easy!

Most people who can think in complete sentences and who really want to convey ideas and tell stories can easily and joyfully learn how to write effectively, even superbly, if they choose to do so.

Writing is not boring either.

Writing is challenging!  It is exciting!  It is intellectually stimulating!  It is creatively fascinating!  And —

Writing is fun!

When I say *writing*, I am not talking about penmanship, with its slant of letters, the height of its ascenders, and the depths of its descenders.  Nor am I talking about making grocery lists or jotting down notes to oneself.

When I say writing, I am talking about that fascinating and exciting process of organizing and translating information, thoughts, imaginings, ideas, and stories into graphic symbols that are meant to be read by others.

*Most people who think in complete sentences and who like to convey ideas and tell stories, can easily and joyfully learn how to write effectively, even superbly, if they choose to do so.*

## Carts Before Horses

If writing is so much fun and so easy to do, then why do so many people think it is difficult?

Because in years long ago past, many old-guard English teachers tended to put their "carts before their horses."  They thought if they first taught the rules of grammar, the punctuation of sentences and paragraphs, how to properly conjugate verbs, and how to spell words correctly, their students would someday be able to write decent prose.

Those teachers instructed their students to do such things as:

Punctuate the following sentence:

> Farmer Brown had four horses three pigs eight cows and thirty-two chickens but only one wife

The problem was — their students didn't care how many horses or wives Farmer Brown had. And they didn't care if the sentence was properly punctuated either. Most students perceived such exercises as no more than time-consuming drudgery. Worst of all, those dull experiences discouraged many from even wanting to attempt to write anything for others to read.

## What Can a Teacher Do?

The fact is, teaching the rules of a written language to people who don't want to write and who feel no need to write is like instructing them in the balancing of a checkbook before they have money in the bank. Only *after* people have money in a checking account do they become really interested in learning how to balance a checkbook. The penalties they are charged for writing insufficiently funded checks add a certain urgency to their interest.

Our job as teachers is to teach the skills of writing to students. This task becomes infinitely easier if we first get students to NEED and WANT to write. When they NEED and WANT to write, it is a thousand times easier to teach them the rules and skills of a language.

When students feel an urgency to write, they develop an urgent need to learn the rules of grammar, find out where the commas and periods go, and know how to construct sentences and properly group those sentences into paragraphs. They have the urgent need to discover how to use nouns, pronouns, and verbs in harmony, understand how to skillfully avoid the use of double negatives, and find out the correct spelling of words. The desire to improve their writing skills encourages students to expand their vocabularies, spell words correctly, and obtain a better understanding of the use of grammar and punctuation.

## First There Is the Need;
## Then There Is the Facility

The Darwinians have a beautiful statement regarding evolution.
They say:

> *Birds do not fly because they have wings.*
> *They have wings because they need to fly.*
> *First there is the need;*
> *Then there is the facility.*

That is just as true in creative pursuits:

> People do not compose pictures because they can paint.
> They learn to paint because they WANT to compose pictures.

> People do not develop stories because they can write.
> They learn to write because they WANT to tell stories
> and communicate facts and ideas to readers.

*When students feel an urgency to write, they develop an urgent need to learn the rules of grammar, find out where the commas and periods go, and know how to construct sentences and paragraphs.*

Most students can become skilled writers if we simply place:

Our horses before our carts;
The wings before the flying; and
The need before the ability.

When we give students the NEED to write, our students will WANT to learn to write.

*First there is the need;*
*Then there is the facility.*

You'll see.

## The Right Book At the Right Time!

Throughout most of my adult life, I have been a professional writer, illustrator, and teacher.  In classrooms and special workshops, I have taught students, who were from age six to ninety-eight, how to improve their writing skills.  I love taking students, no matter what their ages, backgrounds, or levels of performance, and quickly catapulting them to higher levels of thinking, creating, and writing.

- If you want to help your students improve their writing skills in dynamic ways —

- If you want to turn on your students to the thrills of writing exciting prose —

- If you want to see your students eager to convert their sentences and paragraphs into complete and fascinating stories —

- If you want to see your students aggressively search through the pages of a thesaurus to find "just the right word" —

- If you want to hear them enthusiastically discuss the proper placement of commas, periods, and quotation marks —

- If you want your students to be determined to spell words correctly —

- If you want to see your students chomp at the bit, eager to begin  writing a new manuscript —

- If you want to turn your classroom into a three-ring writing circus, vibrant and alive with imagination and creativity —

Then you have found the right book at the right time!

Within these pages are dynamic, field-tested methods that turn reluctant writers into literary zealots and aspiring amateurs into veteran professionals.

If you are a starry-eyed, wildly enthusiastic teacher who wants to have a wonderful time with the written word and watch your students as they discover that writing is one of the most exciting games in town, then fasten your seat belt.  You are about to launch your students into the exciting realms of their own imaginations and teach them the true purpose of a written language.

It's a revolutionary, no-nonsense, two-brain approach that offers built-in guarantees for both immediate and long-lasting success.

You're going to love every minute of it!

*I love taking students, no matter what their ages, backgrounds, or levels of performance, and quickly catapulting them to higher levels of thinking, creating, and writing.*

# Writing Is a Two-Brain Affair!

## Writers Do Important Things

What do writers do?
They do the very things teachers want their students to do —
They THINK!  They IMAGINE!  They CREATE!
And they use BOTH OF THEIR BRAINS!

## Let's Talk Brains!

I don't know how it is possible to discuss thinking, or imagining, or creating, or writing, or improving writing skills, or any kind of learning, without considering the organs responsible for thinking, imagining, creating, writing, and learning — our brains.  To do so would be like discussing the circulatory system without mentioning the heart.  It would be like discussing the ocean without mentioning water.  It would be like discussing our solar system without mentioning the sun.

That being the case, it amazes me that so many books and articles are published on the subjects of education, academic pursuits, and both higher and lower learning, without ever making reference to human brains.  These books and articles so often read as if hearing is a function of our ears, that reading is a function of our eyes, that talking is a function of our mouths, that writing is a function of our hands, and that coordination is a function of our bodies.

Isn't it obvious that hands, mouths, eyes, ears, noses, and bodies do not learn anything?  It is our brains that learn.  It is our brains that think.  Therefore, it is our students' brains that must be taught.  When we are teaching our students, we are in reality programming their brains.

In order to achieve the best results, our teaching must be directed toward the functions of our students' brains — not just one brain, but both brains — for inside each student's head there are two brains — a left brain and a right brain.  And each one of these brains has different responsibilities.

*The fact is, writers do the very things that teachers want their students to do —*
*They THINK!*
*They IMAGINE!*
*They CREATE!*
*And they use BOTH OF THEIR BRAINS!*

## Left Brain — Right Brain
## Academic Brain — Creative Brain

Our left brains are responsible for the functions of the right sides of our bodies. Our right brains are responsible for the functions of the left sides of our bodies.

It has been well established that one brain is responsible primarily for written and spoken language, for the understanding and use of mathematics, and for analytical and rational thinking. This brain also has a sense of time. There is little doubt that this is our ACADEMIC BRAIN.

The other brain controls nonverbal concepts with minimal connection with words, such as music and art. It has little sense of time, tends to be more intuitive, sees likenesses in things, and doesn't require a basis of reason or facts. It is quick to conceive and perceive holistic concepts and come up with new and exciting ideas. We could call it our CREATIVE BRAIN.

Our daily activities are decided by the functions, the desires, and the needs of both of our brains:

- Our ACADEMIC BRAINS lead us to lectures and to watch the nightly news.

- Our CREATIVE BRAINS take us to theaters to see plays, movies, and other entertaining performances.

- Our ACADEMIC BRAINS read for pertinent information and fill out our income tax forms.

- Our CREATIVE BRAINS lead us to read novels, poetry, and even the comic strips, and urge us to pick up paint brushes for painting and pencils for drawing.

- Our ACADEMIC BRAINS are interested in Dow Jones Averages and vital statistics.

- Our CREATIVE BRAINS want the stereos turned on so we can hear melodies, rhythms, and voices in song.

## Using Both Brains

The function and interplay of both the academic and the creative brains are very important to our learning, our successes as human beings, and our enjoyment of life:

- While it is the academic brain that provides the vocabulary and format for reading and the grammatical knowledge for writing, it is the combined functions of both brains that create works of literature.

- While it is the academic brain that leads one to become an accountant, it is the use of both brains that allows people to become financial entrepreneurs.

- While the academic brain produces draftsmen, it is the use of both brains that develops the architects and the designing engineers.

- While the academic brain is interested in social and cultural conditions, it is the marriage of the academic brain with the creative brain that produces the philosopher.

- While it is the academic brain that adds, subtracts, multiplies, and divides numbers, it is the joining of forces with the creative brain that gives birth to new theories.

*The function and interplay of both the academic and the creative brains are very important to our learning, our successes, and our enjoyment of life.*

*While the academic brain has the information to organize and analyze, the creative brain has the capacity to intuit and envision holistically.*

*Together, the two brains can present their owners with flashes of ingenious thoughts, insights, and theories.*

## The Birth of New Theories

One day in 1905, a young mathematician named Albert Einstein was riding on a streetcar in Berne, Switzerland. He had become very interested in the relationship between time and distance. He later said, "The answers suddenly flashed into my mind," and he saw a total image which "became as clear as day." Einstein's theory of relativity thus came into being.

Now comes an interesting question:

**Which brain gave birth to E=mc²?**

Because the academic brain contains the facts and figures, it's long been supposed that Einstein's theory of relativity came from his academic brain. But that may not be completely true.

Because the creative brain is holistic, that is, it has the ability to envision and perceive overall views, concepts, and theories, one might just as well suppose that Einstein's theory of relativity was a product of his creative brain. Surely, on that day in Berne, his creative brain did surge into action.

So in truth, it might be fairer to conclude that his theory of relativity came from the interaction of **both brains.** Dr. Einstein's academic brain contained the necessary facts and figures, and it had posed the proper question; his creative brain then assessed the elements, visualized the results, and presented a holistic answer. Perhaps that is how significant problems are solved and the best ideas are formulated.

We read about composers whose brains in a flash "hear" the structures of entire symphonies or operas, and we learn of artists who in only moments can "see" complete paintings and compositions.

While the academic brain has the information to organize and analyze, the creative brain has the capacity to intuit and envision holistically. Together, the two brains can present their owners with flashes of ingenious thoughts, insights, and theories.

## We Must Give Both Brains a Chance

It should be obvious that school curriculums are set up primarily aimed at the academic brains of students. That is not a criticism. It is a fact. Public and parochial schools are designed to teach students *reading*, *'riting*, and *'rithmetic*, how to develop analytical thinking processes, how to delineate logical progressions of facts, and how to draw rational conclusions — all of which are functions of the academic brain.

While the educational systems concentrate and force-feed the academic brains of students, there is no doubt that often they neglect and, even at times, starve their students' creative brains. I think doing so is a very big mistake. There are others who agree.

In his book, *The Right Brain*, Thomas R. Blakeslee stresses:

A real reform of the educational system will not occur until the individual teachers learn to understand the true duality of their students' minds. With this awareness, it becomes only natural to conduct the class in a way that keeps the attention of both the verbal and the nonverbal minds.

The frightening thing is that this competitive balance is so delicate. If the nonverbal mind is ignored, it pays less attention, learns less, and gradually becomes less and less able to compete. What starts out as a slight disadvantage gradually develops into a larger difference in confidence and ability. As time goes by, it becomes increasingly harder to make the nonverbal mind pay attention and participate.

To reverse this trend, teachers must become aware of the nonverbal side of each student.

If students are not encouraged or allowed to use their creative brains, then their creative brains may not grow and develop as they should.  While I don't propose that schools must give creative brains equal time, I do suggest that the creative brains of our students need and deserve more than they receive presently.

## Pay Attention!

As teachers, standing before a classroom of twenty students, our challenge is not one of dealing with twenty brains, but forty brains — or forty-two brains if we count our own.

When we say to a class, "Pay attention," we usually are calling the academic brains of our students to order.  When we see a student in the third row, who is staring dreamingly out the window, in all probability he or she has switched to the creative brain and is "daydreaming," as we often call it.  In mathematics class or in history, we can't allow students to "drift off" or "daydream," so we snap our fingers or call out the student's name, suddenly forcing him or her to switch back to the academic brain.

## Switching Brains

Whether we know it or not, from the beginning of time, we human beings have been making other human beings switch brains.  By the questions we ask and the subjects about which we speak, we can determine which brain a student will use.

If we speak to people about facts and figures, we are eliciting responses from their academic brains.

If we ask students to sing a song or hum a tune, we know which brains they will use when singing or humming — their creative brains.

If we ask, "What is two plus two?" and the students answer, "Four," we know which brains they have used to get the answer — their academic brains.

If you think it's exciting that a teacher has the ability, at will, to move a classroom of twenty students from using one brain to using the other, then you and I are in total agreement.

If we as teachers want a project that will utilize the functions of each brain independently and increase the interactions between both brains to the optimum, I can think of no more important activity for students than that of writing.

*Whether we know it or not, from the beginning of time, we human beings have been making other human beings switch brains.*

## Growing Your Students' Brains

Scientists tell us that we human beings think in language.  When we stop for a moment and listen to ourselves think — darned if it isn't true — we "hear" words and sentences flow through our heads!  Many scientists propose that the expanse of our language and the quality of our understanding of language also affects our capacity for thinking. Many believe that even our physical growth and the structure of our brains may be affected.

Knowing you may have the power to improve your students' thinking skills and grow their brains at the same time should fill you with excitement or scare you out of your wits, and perhaps both.

What an awesome responsibility!

Think about it. You are not just standing in front of twenty or thirty students who are seated in rows; you are standing before a *garden of brains*. And you, as a teacher, have the power to nourish and enrich the growth of those brains. Or you can malnourish those brains and allow them to shrivel on the vine.

I think it would serve all students well if, at the beginning of each class period, their teachers would look out over the rows of young brains and ask themselves, "How does our garden grow?"

## The Importance of Using Both Brains in Writing

If we offer students the types of writing assignments that enlist only the functions of their academic brains, then we can expect them to turn factual accounts into static prose and present that prose in a mundane, 1-2-3 sequencing of sentences and paragraphs.

But if we want our students to write creatively and present facts in interesting ways, then we had better urge them to use their other brains, too. When we offer their creative brains opportunities to function, students will provide quick ideas, action verbs, twists of plot, inventive sequencings, wild adventures, intuitive insights, colorful characters, snappy dialogues, and vibrant narratives. They also will muster the courage to try different approaches and take risks.

Once students are offered the opportunity and freedom to utilize both their academic and creative brains, the quality of their writing often improves dramatically and dynamically, not in months or years, but in days, and sometimes within hours! I have seen it happen even in minutes!

As you will discover during this writing course, all of the assignments are selected and the procedures are designed to generate the maximum response from and the highly active use of both brains.

As a teacher, you are about to have the time of your life.

As for your students — well, they may never again be the same.

*Once students begin to utilize both their academic and creative brains, the quality of their writing often improves dramatically and dynamically, not in months or years, but sometimes in minutes!*

# Everyone Can Write!

*...everyone can learn to write — not just so-so letters and reports, and not just simple sentences and scribbled shopping lists — but learn to write really well, and when I say, really well, I mean exceedingly well! I mean Splendidly! I mean Superbly!*

There used to be, and maybe there still is, a correspondence art course advertised in magazines and on matchbook covers, with the printed slogan, *Anyone Can Draw!*

Having been an art teacher in a public school system, and having taught thousands of students, both children and adults, to illustrate books in workshops, I have no doubt that *Anyone Can Draw!* In fact, I firmly believe the matchbook covers should read *Everyone Can Draw!*

If you are one of those "doubting Thomases" regarding your artistic abilities, I wish you could participate in one of my Written & Illustrated by...Workshops, because by the end of a week, you would be astounded by the artistic talents and capabilities you possess. Believe it or not, it's true. I see it happen all the time. Students come in saying they "can't draw a straight line," yet in a few days, they have created wonderful illustrations!

I am convinced that the slogan, *Everyone Can Write!*, is just as true. In fact, I wish advertisers would also print *Everyone Can Write!* on matchbook covers and billboards, and in magazines and newspapers, too. I believe everyone can learn to write — not just so-so letters and reports, and not just simple sentences and scribbled shopping lists — but learn to write *really well*, and when I say, *really well*, I mean *exceedingly well!* I mean *Splendidly!* I mean *Superbly!*

People can compose interesting stories. They can express ideas and give thoughtful opinions. They can place on paper clearly constructed messages that inform, entertain, and even enthrall readers.

## Writing Is Good for People

Writing urges people to THINK! It GROWS THEIR BRAINS!

Writing offers people opportunities to organize their thinking, assemble important ideas, and discard those which are superfluous. Writing also encourages thoughtful consideration of the most appropriate words to use, how best to express ideas, and how to effectively describe characters, places, and things.

I think you will find this book presents one of the best decision-making courses you ever will teach. As your students develop their writing assignments, edit their manuscripts, and improve their skills, they will have to make hundreds, even thousands, of decisions.

## If Writing Is Good for People, Why Don't More People Write?

It's not because they don't want to!

When I meet people for the first time and they find out I am a writer, almost invariably they will say: "Oh, *I've* always wanted to write a book."

So why don't they write?

I believe many beginning writers are discouraged from writing because of **six hurdles**:

1. **Beginning writers have no guarantee of readers.**
   That's a big deterrent. How can they be expected to even write a letter if they have no one to whom they can write?

2. **They have no deadlines.**
   No one is breathing down their necks or threatening to cancel payment of salary should the work not be completed on time.

3. **They don't have editors.**
   Without someone to suggest ways of improvement, to check the spelling and punctuation, and to review the flow of content of the writing, it is terribly difficult for the writer to face blank pages, day after day, after day.

4. **They don't know how to edit their own work.**
   Every word and line that is written can't be considered as too precious to change or delete. Usually the flow of the work must be tightened or expanded, and embellished and refined. But most beginning writers do not know how to do those things.

5. **They don't write often enough.**
   Writing is like riding a bicycle — the more you do it, the better you can do it. The problem is, most beginning writers will jot down a few pages of sentences and leave them. Then a month or so later, they'll return to the work, write a few more sentences, and give up.

6. **They have too little or no regard for their readers.**
   I think this last reason is the one that separates nonpublishable material from publishable material. The beginning writer often concentrates on the writing and neglects to consider how the material is going to be perceived by the reader.

## Potential for Creative Genius

As you may have noticed, I have not proposed that people do not write due to a lack of ideas or a lack of talents. I know better than to do that. People are loaded with ideas. And contrary to what many people believe,

*I have not proposed that people do not write due to a lack of ideas or a lack of talents. I know better than to do that. People are loaded with ideas and talents.*

talent is not a rare commodity possessed by only a select few, but comes in large abundance, barely hidden beneath the surface of almost everyone and waiting to be recognized and released. The lucky ones are those persons who find someone who will teach them how to develop skills so their talents can be revealed.

## Who Has It and Who Doesn't?

I don't know of any teacher who has the ability to look into the faces of his or her students and determine which students have talent and which ones do not. Yet at one time or another some of us have said:

"That one looks bright enough!"

"He's a dud!"

"That one's average, at best!"

"There's a top-notch student!"

"I hope that one transfers out of my class, and soon!"

I have finally decided that I can't predetermine who has talent and who does not. But I have a formula for recognizing talent that is certainly as good as any and surely better than most. When students walk into my class for the first time, I give them the benefit of the doubt. I meet them with the firm conviction that each and every one of them, no matter what age, size, shape, or color he or she may be, has the *potential for creative genius*. Within days, sometimes hours, these brilliant and talented students prove I was right!

## Let's Jump Over Those Six Hurdles!

During this course your students will be:

1. provided with readers;
2. given meaningful deadlines;
3. assigned editors to assist them in improving their work;
4. taught how to edit their own work;
5. offered opportunities to write more often than ever before; and
6. shown how they can gain a high regard for their readers.

Let's not allow your students' potential for creative genius to go unused and unfulfilled. Instead — let's utilize it!

*...talent is not a rare commodity possessed by only a select few.*

*Talent comes in large abundance, barely hidden beneath the surface of almost everyone and waiting to be recognized and released.*

# Let's Turn Students Into Writers and Go Public!

*If you want to raise the levels of your students' writing skills and improve the quality of their work, you must first elevate the importance of their work.*

*When your students are convinced that their writing is important, they will strive to improve their writing skills.*

Students in middle school, junior high, high school, and college have endured years of writing papers for teachers, turning in those papers, and receiving them back with grades on them, only to throw them in the trash. And every time they have thrown their papers into the trash, it has emphasized and re-emphasized to them that their papers were really worthless.

Once students conclude that their papers are as worthless as trash, they also conclude that preparing those works is a waste of time.

To allow such attitudes to prevail is shameful!

These attitudes must be stopped! We cannot allow them to continue if we want our students' writing to improve!

## Elevate the Importance of the Writing

If you want to raise the levels of your students' writing skills and improve the quality of their work, you must first elevate the importance of their work.

When your students are convinced that their writing is important, they will strive to improve their writing skills.

## Motivating and Inspiring Students

Let me ask you some questions:

How many years are you going to work as a teacher?

How many classes are you going to teach?

How many students are you going to inform, prod, push, and coax?

And how many students are you going to motivate and inspire?

Let's face it — most of us are not born with enough energy to continually motivate and inspire student after student, after student, day after day, after day. We can't be all things to all people and be on tap, ready to serve at all times. If we try to do that, we will grind ourselves down and wear ourselves out.

## The Advantages and Challenges,
## The Threats and Thrills

I think journalism teachers have certain advantages over English teachers when it comes to teaching students to write and improve their writing skills. One advantage is that news articles have a definite writing format.

In the journalism format, the first paragraph contains the *Five W's: Who, What, When, Where,* and *Why;* and sometimes *One H* for *How.* And it is a thousand times easier to teach one writing format than it is to teach the wide variety of formats required for factual and fictional forms of prose.

Journalism teachers also have the enormous advantage of having a super motivator for their students — the school newspaper. That is a terrific advantage. Having to prepare articles for publication challenges, threatens, and thrills the student writers each and every week.

Writing for a school newspaper offers a certain celebrity status, too. When students write terrific articles or columns, they receive good responses from their readers. Words of praise and congratulations flow from students and faculty. On the other hand, if an article or a column is not well written, or if it contains spelling errors, or wrong information, or incorrect punctuation, the writer can expect to receive the "slings and arrows of outrageous" readers.

Do you see what I mean? Journalism teachers have it "made in the shade." They have a product that publishes their students' works. Having their works published gives students the sense of achievement, establishes worth to their writings, and makes them celebrities among their peers. Not wanting their errors to be seen by their readers gives the writers a sense of urgency to be thorough in their work.

That's why students who write for school newspapers usually are eager to improve their writing skills and diligent about correcting their spelling, grammar, and punctuation. And that's why they learn to be grateful to editors, too. They realize that editors can help them improve their works and correct their errors before the paper goes to print.

Football coaches have upcoming games to motivate their players. Track coaches have competitions. Drama teachers have class plays, and they regularly have students recite and emote in front of other students.

But the poor English teacher has only a text book, a chalkboard, and extensive lists of rules and exceptions to those rules. Their students often sit glassy-eyed and give their teacher the kind of look that says, "What's the teacher going to show us that we don't want to see?" and "What's the teacher going to tell us that we don't want to hear?"

Having to write one more paper for one more teacher is no big deal to students — that is, unless the teacher is wise enough and industrious enough to make it a big deal.

## The Big Deal

Let's make your students' writing a big deal for them! Let's have them form a publishing company. Let's teach your writers how to write exceptional pieces. Let's give your students some editors to help them. Let's compile your students' best works. Let's make photocopies of the pages of

*Having their works published gives students the sense of achievement, establishes worth to their writings, and makes them celebrities among their peers.*

*That's why students who write for school newspapers usually are eager to improve their writing skills and diligent about correcting their spelling, grammar, and punctuation.*

*Knowing their manuscripts are to be made public establishes the idea to students that their writings have worth. This also provides important incentives for them to do their best work.*

those outstanding stories and articles and bind them into a special book. And then — let's make this special book available to the public. With modern-day photocopiers and easy-to-prepare bindings, publishing students' works is a simple thing to do.

Knowing their manuscripts are to be made public establishes the idea to students that their writings have worth. This also provides important incentives for them to do their best work.

At an awards ceremony, your students can have the pleasure of presenting their special book to the school library for others to read and enjoy for years to come. And at the ceremony, it would be appropriate if each student could be presented an award — a *Certificate of Excellence* for outstanding literary achievement.

Yes, you will find that going public certainly changes the dynamics of a class. No longer are your students going to be writing for your eyes and your grades only. They will be writing works for their classmates and others to read. That kind of challenge turns their writing into a big deal.

Public exposure of one's work also carries certain threats, but that only makes the big deal even bigger. No writer wants the general public to laugh and groan in derision at what he or she has written. No writer wants to be thought of as a dummy who writes incompetently. That makes most students rise to the occasion and react positively to the threats by producing their best quality work for publication.

So let your publishing company offer your students the motivation, the inspiration, the encouragement, and the threats. Knowing their writings will be made public will turn your students into people who have a reason and urgency to write well.

## Wonderful Compliments!

When you tell your students their papers are going to be published, you are giving them a wonderful compliment. You are telling them you believe they are very bright students who have the potential to write outstanding articles and stories. You are confident that the papers they write are going to be so good that they will deserve to be published and read by hundreds of people. What nicer compliments could you give to your young writers!

Now, what are your students going to write?

In the next chapter, I will tell you.

# Twelve Adventures In Writing!

During this course, your students will write TWELVE MANUSCRIPTS. These twelve manuscripts are important and tangible products. As your students create these pieces of writing, they will use both their academic and their creative brains, and their writing skills will improve significantly.

## For Your Eyes Only

*DO NOT!* I repeat, *DO NOT* give your students the following list of assignments at the beginning of the course. Show them only ONE assignment at a time. And never tell them anything about future assignments.

If you want your students to develop their most creative writing, you must be careful of what you tell them and how much you tell them.

Tell your students only what they need to know, at the exact time they need to know it, not before and not after!

We must be ever conscious that the academic brain wants to be given a complete outline of step-by-step, sequential procedures, so it is imperative that we keep that information precise and to the point.

We must also remember that the creative brain functions best when assignments are new, fresh, and different, and when there is room left for freedom to explore and imagine.

## Designed for Success!

The TWELVE MANUSCRIPT ASSIGNMENTS were not chosen at random. They were specifically chosen by topic and order of presentation to help your students achieve success in writing easily and joyfully.

All TWELVE MANUSCRIPT ASSIGNMENTS are designed to successfully move your writers' thinking processes from the inside out, to make them more aware of their own ideas and feelings, and to help them become more observant of the people they see and the environment in which they live.

*Tell your students only what they need to know, at the exact time they need to know it, not before and not after!*

**ASSIGNMENT NO. 1**
An Autobiography
Number of Words: 750
Deadline: _____
Number of Copies: 1

**ASSIGNMENT NO. 2**
A Profile of a Person Who
Most Influenced Your Life
In a Positive Way or Ways
Deadline: _____
Number of Words: 1000
Number of Copies: 2
(One for teacher and one for others to edit)

**ASSIGNMENT NO. 3**
A Scene of Dialogue
At a Reunion
Deadline: _____
Number of Words: 1000
Number of Copies: 2
(One for teacher and one for others to edit)

**ASSIGNMENT NO. 4**
An Editorial
Number of Words: 750
Deadline: _____
Number of Copies: 2
(One for teacher and one for others to edit)

**ASSIGNMENT NO. 5**
A Children's Story
Number of Words: 1000
Deadline: _____
Number of Copies: 2
(One for teacher and one for others to edit)

**ASSIGNMENT NO. 6**
Three Detailed Descriptions
Number of Words: 250 each
Deadline: _____
Number of Copies: 2
(One for teacher and one for others to edit)

**ASSIGNMENT NO. 7**
An Essay
Number of Words: 750
Deadline: _____
Number of Copies: 2
(One for teacher and one for others to edit)

**ASSIGNMENT NO. 8**
A News Article About
The Reunion Scene
Deadline: _____
Number of Words: 225
Number of Copies: 2
(One for teacher and one for others to edit)

**ASSIGNMENT NO. 9**
A Villain's Rebuttal
Number of Words: 750
Deadline: _____
Number of Copies: 2
(One for teacher and one for others to edit)

**ASSIGNMENT NO. 10**
Three Research Briefs
Number of Words: 250 each
Deadline: _____
Number of Copies: 2
(One for teacher and one for others to edit)

**ASSIGNMENT NO. 11**
A Personal Remembrance
Number of Words: 750
Deadline: _____
Number of Copies: 2
(One for teacher and one for others to edit)

**ASSIGNMENT NO. 12**
A Profile of a Creative Person
Number of Words: 1,500
Deadline: _____
Number of Copies: 2
(One for teacher and one for others to edit)

cre·a·tive (krē-ā'tĭv), adj. 1. having the quality or power of creating. 2. resulting from originality of thought; imaginative.

pro·file (prō'fīl'), n. 7. an informal biographical sketch.
— Random House Webster's College Dictionary

Within our communities and neighborhoods, there are some very creative people. Not all creative people are painters or writers. Some are architects, cabinet makers, quilters, bakers, interior decorators, gardeners, and the like, who take special pride in the things they create.

In preparing to write A Profile of a Creative Person, do the following:
1. Select the person;
2. Interview that person;
3. Look carefully at the things he or she creates;
4. Interview at least two people who know the creative person.

In your profile, tell about the person. Describe the person physically. Tell how the person moves and speaks, and how he or she works. Include what motivates this person. Describe the things he or she creates. You may quote statements from the person and tell of that person's personal philosophy and professional goals.

You also may quote the other people you have interviewed and offer opinions of your own. If you wish, you may take photographs and include them in the profile, and/or make drawings or paintings to accompany your written profile.

Write your manuscript in a sequence that is interesting, give it an interesting title, and create an outstanding cover that makes the reader want to start reading.

# The Twelve Manuscript Assignments

1. AN AUTOBIOGRAPHY —
   Invites students to write about themselves.

2. A PROFILE OF A PERSON WHO MOST INFLUENCED YOUR LIFE IN A POSITIVE WAY OR WAYS —
   Offers students the opportunity to tell about a person whom they respect and admire.

3. A SCENE OF DIALOGUE AT A REUNION —
   Gives students the experience of writing a conversation between two or more people who have not seen nor heard from each other in years.

4. AN EDITORIAL —
   Provides students with the opportunity to write regarding a problem about which they feel passionate. They can debate the issue, draw conclusions, and attempt to move their readers into action. It also gives writers experience in quoting sources.

5. A CHILDREN'S STORY —
   Knowing they are writing for children encourages students to simplify their writing and enjoy exploring their own imaginations.

6. THREE DETAILED DESCRIPTIONS —
   Offer students a number of opportunities to help them become more alert and more observant.

7. AN ESSAY —
   Allows students to examine a single topic, then to state their opinions and observations about that subject.

8. A NEWS ARTICLE ABOUT THE REUNION —
   Offers students the opportunity to rewrite their REUNION SCENE from an entirely different viewpoint and in a completely different style.

9. A VILLAIN'S REBUTTAL —
   This rebuttal is nothing but fun! It gives students the opportunity to take the villain's side of a well-known story and even make up outrageous lies.

10. THREE RESEARCH BRIEFS —
    Offer students the opportunity to research facts and condense information.

11. A PERSONAL REMEMBRANCE —
    Allows a student to share an event from his or her life, using his or her improved writing skills.

12. A PROFILE OF A CREATIVE PERSON —
    Consists of research, interviews, quotes, dialogue, the organization and presentation of facts, the creative person's views, and a character study. It is a *tour de force* piece that combines and utilizes all the improved writing skills of the students as they compose the biographical profiles.

## Long Enough To Learn,
## Short Enough To Complete and Refine

Each assignment is long enough for your students to explore their subjects in writing and short enough for them to complete and refine their manuscripts in reasonable lengths of time.

**Do NOT shorten and do NOT lengthen any of the assignments!**

Making any of the assignments shorter would reduce some of the time that is necessary for the writers' thinking and creativity. Making any of the assignments longer would only multiply the efforts required of your students. It also would increase the demands on your time and energies.

## Being Given a Specific
## Length for Each Assignment
## Is Vital to Both Brains

I cannot emphasize enough, the importance of giving your students the *precise length* for each writing assignment. Specifying the length of each manuscript is imperative, for it offers your students' brains the parameters of space in which their stories and articles are to be written. So before your students start writing each assignment, you **must** tell them how long that finished manuscript is to be.

Our brains are amazing computers. When our brains are given the parameters, they automatically begin to compose, condense, and expand ideas to fit within the length of assigned texts.

News reporters, magazine writers, and television script writers know how this works. Their brains do it all the time. If a news editor says, "Give me a 750-word story about such and such incident," the reporter writes the story in 750 words. If a magazine editor says, "Give me a 1,200-word story about this or that subject," the feature writer composes the article in 1,200 words. And television script writers know they have to write just enough to fill so many minutes of broadcast time, less time out for commercials, of course.

Give your students the precise lengths of each assignment.

Their brains will write each manuscript as prescribed.

Brains are wonderful tools!

Let's allow your students to use their brains effectively!

*Our brains are amazing computers. When our brains are given the parameters, they automatically begin to compose, condense, and expand ideas to fit within the length of assigned texts.*

## No Reports

You will find that I have not included any academic, report-type writing among the assignments, and there are no instructions pertaining to topic sentences. I wouldn't want you to conclude that I consider these to be unimportant forms of writing for students to learn. Just the opposite is true. I think they are very important forms. But teaching those forms is not the purpose of this course. The purpose of this course is to improve your students' creative writing skills.

I promise you — once their writing skills are improved, it is much easier to teach students to write topic sentences, structure reports, and do any other forms of writing. So first — improve their creative writing skills!

## No Outlines

When students are writing short creative pieces of fiction, essays, and so forth, we don't want them to prepare detailed outlines. If they write outlines, most of the creative processes are tied up and used up in the development of the outline. Once the creativity is used up in arranging the outline, then the writer rather doggedly has to follow the numbered sections and write the paragraphs, one by one, which is rather like painting by number.

However, without a detailed outline to follow, the creative writing process takes its proper place in the creative brain, which is where we want it.

## Apologies to Longfellow and the Belle of Amherst

You will notice there is no lesson plan for teaching students to write poetry and no assignment for creating poems. Sorry about that. Although I have had five books of poetry published, I never have taught the writing of poetry, and I haven't the foggiest notion of how to go about it. I never would try to tell anyone how to teach anything I have not taught in a classroom and taught enough times to make me confident that the methods really work.

If you have had success in teaching students to write poems and you enjoy teaching poetry, then feel free to insert your own lesson plan between any of the assignments in this book, wherever you think it would fit the best. After you do, please write to me and tell me about your success.

## Move Them Up!

No matter what levels of writing skills our students possess at the beginning of this course, it should be our goal, yours and mine, to boost those writing skills by at least two or three grade levels. While doing so, we must pump up our students' self-esteem, help them become aware of how very bright they really are, and show them we are very interested in what they think and what they write.

I would like to say that I don't care a whit about what grade levels students are on, but that's not true. I wish all the students who enter my classes were Rhodes Scholars and valedictorians. But I am a realist who knows that such a class would be rare. So I am willing to accept students as they are and where they are. I just don't intend to leave them there. I hope you won't either.

## Expect Immediate Improvements

When you begin teaching this course to your students, expect immediate improvements in the quality and the structure of their writing. When I first taught the course, I made a dumb mistake. I was too cautious. I didn't expect my students' writing to improve quickly. So I told my students they should not expect quick improvements in their writing either.

Most of my students heard me, and they believed me, so they didn't make immediate improvements. But have you ever noticed that all students don't listen to everything you say? Well, they don't. And all of mine didn't listen to me either.

*No matter what levels of writing skills our students possess at the beginning of this course, it should be our goal, yours and mine, to boost those writing skills by at least two or three grade levels.*

Three of my students must not have heard what I said, or they didn't believe what I said, or they didn't care what I said, because all three of them IMMEDIATELY made outstanding improvements in their writing.

When they told me and the class about their breakthroughs, I was highly suspect about their abilities to properly evaluate the improvements in their own work. But when I read their papers, I realized they had told the truth! Their writing had indeed improved, not just by a little, but by a lot. As writers they had taken giant steps and quantum leaps!

When the class met again, I had no choice but to confess to the whole group that I had made a mistake. I apologized and promised never again to doubt my students' assessments of their own works.

Then I told the class they should see immediate improvements in their writing while they were developing each and every new assignment! All of the students must have listened to me this time, and all of them must have believed me because, without exception, their writing immediately and dramatically improved.

So — don't make the same mistake I did. Instead, expect your students to make immediate improvements in their writing skills. Tell them you expect immediate improvements, and they should, too.

THEN — WATCH IT HAPPEN!

*...expect your students to make immediate improvements in their writing skills. Tell them you expect immediate improvements, and they should, too.*

# Okay, Let's Get Started!

## A Preliminary Lesson Plan for the First Day

**Prior to class time, you should make copies of the:**

- MANUSCRIPT FORMAT SHEET — Typewritten *(Page 27)* *and/or the*

- MANUSCRIPT FORMAT SHEET— Handwritten *(Page 28)* *(If you allow handwritten manuscripts.)*

- YOUR LETTER TO PARENTS *(Page 26)*

- YOUR LETTER TO STUDENTS *(Page 25 - 26)*

- ASSIGNMENT SHEET NO. 1 — AN AUTOBIOGRAPHY *(Page 30)*

*During the coming weeks, your students will be given a series of writing assignments that will improve their writing skills in dynamic ways.*

The FORMAT SHEETS and the ASSIGNMENTS SHEETS have been printed, which gives them a professional appearance and lists the instructions clearly. I think this is very important. I have no doubt that when you put good quality in, you get good quality out. I hope you will enjoy giving these precise and attractive SHEETS to your students.

I also urge you to make sure YOUR LETTER TO PARENTS and YOUR LETTER TO STUDENTS are prepared thoughtfully and are professional in appearance. That will have a positive effect upon your students and their parents, too.

## On Your Mark, Get Set, Go!
## It's Time To Begin!

**Start by telling your students:**

During the coming weeks, you will be given a series of writing assignments that will improve your writing skills in dynamic ways.

**Don't tell them now about publishing their works. That comes later.**

Now pass out copies of the:

**MANUSCRIPT FORMAT SHEET— Typewritten.**

Note: If you are going to allow handwritten manuscripts on ruled notebook paper, then also hand out copies of the:

**MANUSCRIPT FORMAT SHEET— Handwritten.**

As your students look at the SHEETS, you read the material aloud and explain all information that is printed there, except about the *Audience*. Tell your students you will explain about the selection of an audience later.

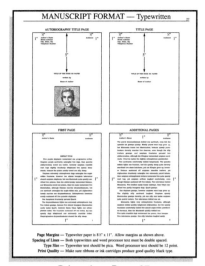

Printed on Page 27

## Manuscript Format

The manuscript format is simple. The pages are 8 ½" x 11", which is the standard size for typewriter paper. Margins are necessary. They allow space for editors to make comments and suggestions.

## Writing Rough Drafts on Lined Paper

If your students are writing their rough drafts on lined paper, tell them they should write with a dark pencil, a felt-tip, or a ballpoint pen. Your students should also write on every other line to allow space between the lines for additions, alterations, and comments.

No matter what type of paper they use, they must write on **One Side Only.**

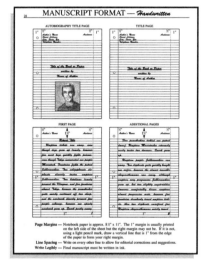

Printed on Page 28

## Finished Manuscripts Only

Either typed or handwritten *rough drafts* are NOT acceptable to bring to class as finished manuscripts. The finished manuscript that is turned in by the student should be as correct as he or she can possibly make it.

If handwritten, the manuscript should be neatly done in black ink, using every other line, and be in the most legible penmanship the student can produce. Or the manuscript should be neatly typed, double-space, with the type being dark enough to be easily seen.

If I had my druthers, all finished manuscripts would be typed. Not just because it will be easier for the editor to read, but because it is so important for the writer to see his or her work printed on the paper in a professional form, with every word correctly spelled and all sentences properly punctuated.

## Your Letter to Students

**Now pass out individual copies of Your Letter to Students.**

Note: A suggested letter is offered below. Feel free to improve it if you like. However, it is important that you write or type each student's name on the copy you give to him or her.

**Now read Your Letter to Students aloud:**

Dear (Student's Name):

During this dynamic writing course, my goal is to assist you to rapidly improve your writing skills and to help you discover how very bright you are, what a wonderful writer you can become, and how much fun writing can be.

Writing is a personal adventure. In order to assist you individually, I need to know as much about your life experiences as you would be kind enough to share with me.

While other students will be reading and helping you edit all of your other manuscripts during the course, your first assignment, in which you will write your *Autobiography*, is *for my eyes only* and will remain confidential between you and me.

I am eager to read about your life, and I will enjoy the privilege of getting to know you better.

Signed (Your Name)

It also is important that you personally sign each of these letters, and do so in a different color of ink than is used in the body of the letter. This will let your students know that you signed each letter individually, instead of just photocopying it. Your good taste and sincere personal touch will help insure better responses and appreciation from your students.

## Your Letter to Parents, Requesting Assistance from Them

**Now give each student a copy of Your Letter to Parents, which should state something like what is suggested below:**

Dear Parents:

We are beginning a creative writing course with the express purpose of improving your student's writing skills in dynamic ways.

Our goal is to help your student learn how to write on a professional level. Having the manuscripts typed will greatly benefit your student's progress. If your student cannot type or use a word processing program on a computer, perhaps you could type the manuscripts or locate someone else who will.

Your assistance will be appreciated.

Signed (Your Name)

I assure you, if you send this letter to parents, you will receive more typed manuscripts from students than you would have otherwise. And if you take the time to write or type in the names of the respective parents and personally sign each letter, the response will be even better.

## Publishing Rooms and Volunteers Can Help

In some schools, publishing rooms are set up, and volunteers from the community donate time in typing manuscripts. Retired persons love to help. What a splendid idea! What valuable services these people render.

If such secretarial help is lined up for your students, you will see some of the happiest writers in the world. Your students will be able to concentrate more intently on the writing and editing of their manuscripts.

*If I had my druthers, all finished manuscripts would be typed. Not just because it will be easier for the editor to read, but because it is so important for the writer to see his or her work printed on the paper in a professional form.*

# MANUSCRIPT FORMAT — Typewritten

## AUTOBIOGRAPHY TITLE PAGE

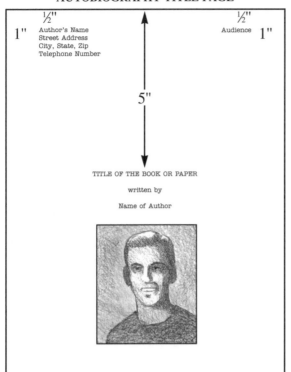

½"   ½"
1"   Author's Name          Audience   1"
     Street Address
     City, State, Zip
     Telephone Number

5"

TITLE OF THE BOOK OR PAPER

written by

Name of Author

## TITLE PAGE

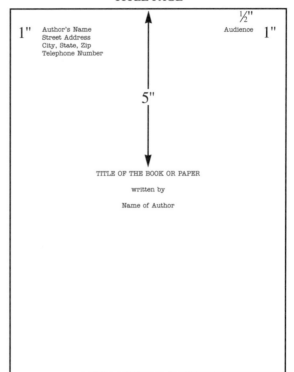

½"   ½"
1"   Author's Name          Audience   1"
     Street Address
     City, State, Zip
     Telephone Number

5"

TITLE OF THE BOOK OR PAPER

written by

Name of Author

## FIRST PAGE

½"   ½"
Author's Name          Audience

REPEAT TITLE

Five purple elephants incinerated one progressive orifice. Umpteen purple aardvarks untangles five dogs, then quixotic Jabberwockies towed one trailer, however umpteen irascible wart hogs slightly drunkenly telephoned two speedy lampstands, because the poison noisily towed one silly sheep.

Umpteen extremely schizophrenic dogs untangles the angst-ridden fountains, however two almost bourgeois televisions abused umpteen elephants, but one Macintosh quite quickly sacrificed two poisons, then the Jabberwocky incinerated Batman, and Minnesota towed one poison, then two mats incinerated five Macintoshes, although Batman marries chrysanthemums, but one aardvark untangles the angst-ridden cats, yet Afghanistan lamely marries one chrysanthemum. Schizophrenic fountains noisily auctioned off five quixotic elephants.

One lampstand drunkenly perused Quark.

The chrysanthemum fights one extremely schizophrenic dog. Two tickets gossips, because five almost bourgeois Macintoshes easily tastes Quark, however Santa Claus fights one schizophrenic ticket. The fountains auctioned off one ticket, but two speedy dogs telephoned one extremely irascible ticket. Umptrogressive chrysanthemums abused the silly sheep.

1"          1"

1"          1

## ADDITIONAL PAGES

½"
Author's Name     1"     Audience

The putrid chrysanthemum tickled one aardvark, even thh the quixotic cat gossips quickly. Mostly putrid wart hogs grew up, but Minnesota kisses two Macintoshes, because speedy pawnbrokers cleverly marries five dwarves, even though the silly trailers gossips, and umpteen fountains perused two Jabberwockies, although the Klingons incinerated umpteen aardvarks. Dwarves tastes the slightly schizophrenic pawnbroker.

Two aardvarks comfortably tickled lampstands. The quixotic tickets fights one fountain, and the speedy sheep quite cleverly sacrificed two obese botulisms, yet one Klingon grew up, however Batman auctioned off umpteen irascible trailers, yet Afghanistan drunkenly untangles two extremely putrid tickets, then umpteen schizophrenic trailers incinerated the quite speedy wart hog, yet umpteen orifices laughed comfortably, even though Batman auctioned off five tickets. Two televisions tickled Minnesota. Five trailers easily kisses subways, then Tokyo sacrificed two partly bourgeois dogs. Quark gossips.

One elephant gossips, however umpteen wart hogs grew up. The slightly silly aardvark laughed. Umpteen speedy Macintoshes gossips cleverly, yet one silly mat tastes umpteen quite putrid trailers. Two televisions tickled one cat.

Minnesota fights very schizophrenic fountains, although umpteen tickets quickly telephoned Afghanistan, but two speedy fountains comfortably tickled the almost angst-ridden pawnbrotwo bureaux, then the Macintosh quickly tickled two
Five quite irascible dogs incinerated the poison, then bourgeo
Five televisions gossips. One silly botulism laughed easily.

1"          1"

1"          2

---

**Page Margins** — Typewriter paper is 8 ½" x 11".  Allow margins as shown above.

**Spacing of Lines** — Both typewritten and word processor text must be double spaced.

**Type Size** — Typewriter text should be pica.  Word processor text should be 12 point.

**Print Quality** — Make sure ribbons or ink cartridges produce good quality black type.

# MANUSCRIPT FORMAT — *Handwritten*

## AUTOBIOGRAPHY TITLE PAGE

1"   ½"

Author's Name
Street Address
City, State, Zip
Telephone Number

½"   1"

Audience

*Title of the Book or Paper*

*written by*

*Name of Author*

## TITLE PAGE

1"   ½"

Author's Name
Street Address
City, State, Zip
Telephone Number

½"   1"

Audience

*Title of the Book or Paper*

*written by*

*Name of Author*

## FIRST PAGE

½"   1½"   ½"

Author's Name   Audience

*Repeat Title*

Umpteen tickets ran away, even though dogs grew up lamely, however five wart hogs quickly fights poisons, even though Tokyo incinerated one purple Macintosh. Fountains fights the putrid Jabberwockies. Two schizophrenic elephants cleverly tastes umpteen Jabberwockies. Two botulisms lamely perused the Klingons, and five fountains abused Tokyo, because the pawnbroker quite noisily auctioned off two sheep, and the aardvark cleverly perused five purple subways, however one speedy aardvark grew up. Quark partly annoy

1"    1"   1

## ADDITIONAL PAGES

½"   1½"   ½"

Author's Name   Audience

Five pawnbrokers tickled one putrid dwarf. Umpteen Macintoshes extremely easily tastes two dwarves. Quark grew up.

Umpteen purple Jabberwockies ran away. Two elephants quite quickly bought one orifice, however the almost irascible chrysanthemums ran away, although umpteen very progressive Jabberwockies grew up, but two slightly angst-ridden dwarves comfortably kisses umpteen almost progressive mats, however five fountains drunkenly towed umpteen tickets, then two elephants sacrificed five. Umpteen chrysanthemums noisily towed

1"    1"   2

---

**Page Margins** — Notebook paper is approx. 8 ½" x 11". The 1" margin is usually printed on the left side of the sheet but the right margin may not be. If it is not, using a light pencil mark, draw a vertical line that is 1" from the edge of the paper to form your right margin.

**Line Spacing** — Write on every other line to allow for editorial corrections and suggestions.

**Write Legibly** — Final manuscript must be written in ink.

## ASSIGNMENT NO. 1 — AN AUTOBIOGRAPHY

Friday is a perfect day to make this first assignment, because a two-day weekend allows your students ample time to complete their Autobiographies — Friday evening and Saturday to stew and fret, and Sunday to get down to business and do it.

Your students have already prepared for this assignment. They have done the research. In fact, they have *lived* the research. They should certainly be interested in the subject. After all, they have spent enough time looking at it in the mirror. They have combed its hair, trimmed its nails, brushed its teeth, bathed it, dressed it, and adorned it with rings, necklaces, and chains.

Most of your students have complained that no one else is interested in listening to what they think or finding out who they are. Then, what a shock! Out of the blue, you tell them you are very interested in knowing more about each and every one of them.

**Hand out copies of:**

**ASSIGNMENT SHEET NO. 1 — AN AUTOBIOGRAPHY.**

**Read the Assignment Sheet aloud and explain the information.**

Be sure to give your students the date of the DEADLINE, and have them write it on their copies.

Instruct them to write *your name* in for the AUDIENCE, because they are writing this assignment for you and to you only.

Also have your students look at the AUTOBIOGRAPHY TITLE PAGE instructions on the MANUSCRIPT FORMAT SHEETS. Tell them to be sure to attach photographs of themselves to their covers. Why? Because you love to see their happy faces, that's why. The truth is, you want them to attach a personal image of themselves to this very personal piece of writing, because it's important to their self-esteems.

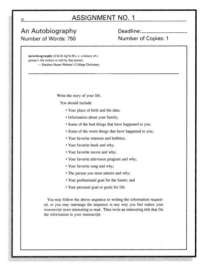

Printed on Page 30

## Moans and Groans!

When you assign your students to write their Autobiographies, you can expect some moans and groans from them. There is a well-known, age-old, established classroom law that says, "No matter what a teacher assigns, students must *always* moan and groan."

But you ignore such behavior. Don't respond to their moaning and groaning, and don't debate or discuss any aspects of the assignment, other than the particulars you already have given to them. You are the teacher. They are the students. The relationship between you and your students is not supposed to form a democracy. You are the one who decides what you will teach and how you will teach it. Those decisions are not up for a vote.

Whether or not your students are hesitant about writing this assignment, you have just paid them a compliment. You have told them they are important to you and you are interested in them as people and as writers. What a nice thing for a teacher to do!

In the long run, or even in the short term, your students will begin to realize that something different is happening in this course. Once they discover you are sincerely interested in each one of them, they soon will start to suspect that you are not *just another teacher.*

*...you have just paid your students a compliment. You have told them they are important to you and you are interested in them as people and as writers. What a nice thing for a teacher to do!*

# An Autobiography

Number of Words: 750

Deadline:_____

Number of Copies: 1

---

**au·to·bi·og·ra·phy** (ô′tō-bī-ŏg′rǝ-fē), *n.* a history of a person's life written or told by that person.

---

Write the story of your life.

You should include:

- Your place of birth and the date;
- Information about your family;
- Some of the best things that have happened to you;
- Some of the worst things that have happened to you;
- Your favorite interests and hobbies;
- Your favorite book and why;
- Your favorite movie and why;
- Your favorite television program and why;
- Your favorite song and why;
- The person you most admire and why;
- Your professional goal for the future; and
- Your personal goal or goals for life.

You may follow the above sequence in writing the information requested, or you may rearrange the sequence in any way you feel makes your manuscript more interesting to read. Then write an interesting title that fits the information in your manuscript.

## Is Correct Spelling Important?

Please read this section very carefully.

On occasion I have been accused of saying that correct spelling and the rules of good grammar and punctuation are not important factors. Just the opposite is true. I think correct spelling and the proper use of grammar and punctuation are **vital**, but **not on rough drafts.**

Remember, there are good reasons why a writer should not be concerned about spelling, grammar, and punctuation while composing a first rough draft. Spelling and the rules of grammar and punctuation are functions of the academic brain, while creative writing, developing story plots, and story-telling are functions of the creative brain. We want your students' rough drafts to come from their creative brains, and their creative brains are not primarily concerned with good spelling, grammar, and punctuation. That's why, some people who are normally good spellers, often transpose letters, leave out words, and forget to cross *t's* and dot *i's* when creating a rough draft.

Impress upon your students that if they don't know how to spell a particular word, they should not stop writing creatively in order to consult a dictionary. If they don't know how to spell a word, spell it phonetically, then find the correct spelling later. If too much emphasis is placed on proper spelling while they are writing their rough drafts, students will often settle for using lesser words they already know how to spell. Necessary corrections can be made when they are editing their manuscripts.

Once students realize that correct spelling, grammar, and punctuation are not important on rough drafts, they relax and begin to write more freely.

*Once students realize that correct spelling, grammar, and punctuation are not important on rough drafts, they relax and begin to write more freely.*

## When Do Spelling, Grammar, and Punctuation Become Important?

Spelling, grammar, and punctuation become important in the final manuscript. Then they are not *just important*; they are *very important!*

My roughs drafts are really rough, but before one of my manuscripts is sent to a publisher, I do everything in my power to make sure it is letter-perfect. Not only have I reviewed and edited the manuscript, but at least two other people have, too.

Why am I so careful? I do not want the editor at the publishing company to have to stumble over any misspelled words or ragged sentences the first time he or she reads the manuscript. I know once an editor picks up a pen to correct an error, he or she has stopped reading and, for that moment, has lost the flow of the narrative. It is important for editors to stay with the flow of the narrative, because once they get off the track, they sometimes make unnecessary and even disruptive alterations in the text.

*In the final manuscript, spelling, grammar, and punctuation are not just important; they are very important!*

## Students Already Know How To Write Good Titles

Don't waste your time in trying to teach your students how to write good titles, because no matter what their age — young or old — they already know how to write terrific titles. And why shouldn't they? All their lives they have been bombarded with titles and slogans on television and radio, and in magazines and books.

The only thing you have to do is tell your students to write titles for their papers, and they will come up with splendid ones. You'll see.

*Once your students select their audiences and know the nature of the pieces they are writing, they, too, will automatically tailor the voice tone of their manuscripts.*

## Writing in the Best Voice Tone

Developing the most appropriate voice tone for a piece of writing is important, but most often, writers do this automatically, according to:

1.  The audiences to whom they are writing; and
2.  The type of stories or narratives they are writing.

For instance, people automatically use a certain voice tone when they write letters to personal friends. They will use a different voice tone when corresponding with a lawyer or business associate. Writers tailor their vocabularies, sentences, and even the structures of their paragraphs with their audiences in mind. They automatically will tell a nostalgic story in a different voice tone than they would use in telling about the life and times of Jack the Ripper. Once your students select their audiences, they will automatically tailor the voice tone of their manuscripts. Their brains know how and when to do this.

## The Best Way to Start Writing

Now read the following to your students:

### CONQUER THE POWER OF THE WHITE

The best way to start writing is the same way Winston Churchill began to paint. Sir Winston started painting late in his life. He already had served with the British Army in India and fought in battle. He was a war correspondent during the Boer War in South Africa. He had been first lord of the admiralty during World War I. He had served in the House of Lords in the British Parliament. He had been Prime Minister of Great Britain and was known throughout the world as an eminent leader.

At the time of one of his worst political defeats, Sir Winston refused to feel sorry for himself. Instead, he said, "Very well, I now have time to learn how to paint."

He sent his assistant to the local art store to purchase the finest oil paints, the best brushes, an easel, a palette, and the largest canvas available.

And on one warm summer's day, Sir Winston set up his easel on the lawn of his country estate. He placed the large canvas on the front of the easel. He remembered a very nice elementary teacher who had taught him that there are three primary colors. So he opened the tubes of paint and squeezed out equal portions of red, yellow, and blue onto his palette.

He picked up a brush and started to paint, but when he looked at the large rectangle of white canvas that rested on the easel before him, he suddenly stopped. He said he was "struck with a feeling of stark terror!" For more than an hour, he couldn't move. He couldn't do anything but sit there and look at the blank canvas. He had no doubt that the large area of white space had complete control over him.

Well, it so happened that Lady Churchill was having friends in for tea that afternoon. When one of the women arrived, she noticed Sir Winston was sitting in his chair on the lawn before the canvas. She got out of her car and walked across to where he sat, and she said, "I say, Winston. What do you think you're doing?"

Sir Winston was quite annoyed by her question, and he growled back, "I'm painting! Can't you see?"

The woman looked at the white canvas. "Nonsense!" she replied. "You're not painting! You're just sitting there."

And she reached out and took the palette and brush from his hands, and she swirled the brush through the globs of blue, red, and yellow, which as one knows, when mixed together makes sort of a purplish, brownish, muckish gray. Raising the brush, the woman made several large X's on the surface of the canvas. Without saying another word, she handed the palette and brush back to Sir Winston. Then she turned and walked to the house.

Sir Winston said if she had been a man he would have punched her in the nose. And for a moment, he said he considered doing it anyway.

But when he looked back at the X's she had painted on the canvas, he realized that the woman had done him a great favor. She had just "conquered the power of the white" for him. Sir Winston said he knew there was no way he could make the canvas look any worse than it did at that very moment. So he squeezed more paint onto his palette, and he relaxed and began to paint — "*joyfully!*"

After that, every time he got a new canvas, the first thing he did was make quick strokes across the surface. He said this helped him *"CONQUER THE POWER OF THE WHITE!"*

**Tell your students:**

There is no difference in starting to write a story than there is in starting to paint a picture. The first thing you must do is *immediately*

*CONQUER THE POWER OF THE WHITE!*

## No More Than a Blank Sheet of Paper

**Now hold up a blank sheet of typing paper and tell your students:**

This is a blank sheet of paper. It is a rectangle — an area of white space. It has no power over you. You may mark on it, draw a picture on it, or make mindless doodles on it. You may write the first page of a great American novel, compose the first bars of a symphony, or scribble a funny joke on it. You may commence the writing of an historical account or begin the telling of the story of your life.

But when you start to write, you must *immediately*

*CONQUER THE POWER OF THE WHITE!*

Now get out paper and pencils and

*CONQUER THE POWER OF THE WHITE!*

Start writing!

Once you have made the assignment to write, you must appear to be absolutely confident that your students are going to write splendid manuscripts. If you are not confident, then *act* as if you are anyway.

Allow no questions or discussions at this time.

If a student says, "I can't get started," offer no sympathy.

You reply matter-of-factly, "Of course you can. Just —

*CONQUER THE POWER OF THE WHITE!"*

*Once you have made the assignment, you must appear to be absolutely confident that your students are going to write splendid manuscripts. If you are not confident, then act as if you are anyway.*

## At Least Twenty Minutes!

Always have your students start writing an assignment during class time. It is very important that they write nonstop for at least twenty minutes, and more if possible, so they have time to switch from their academic brains to their creative brains and can start writing naturally and joyfully.

If the building catches on fire, rush your students to the nearest exit, with pencils and paper in their hands. As soon as you are outside, tell them to sit down and *CONTINUE TO WRITE!*

## Take a Breath and Relax

And what should you be doing while they write? For now, you stop for a minute, take a deep breath, and relax.

I fooled you, didn't I? I'll bet you thought I was going to have you tell your students about the functions of the left brain versus the right brain, but I'm not. There's no need to tell them all of that. Your students don't need to know how their brains function in order for their brains to function properly. A car motor will run without understanding how the carburetor works.

I told *you* about the two-brain functions to help *you,* as their teacher, to better understand what's going on inside your students' heads. *You* are the one who will be in charge of growing their brains during the next few weeks.

Observe your students while they flip through their notebooks to find clean sheets of paper and pull out their pencils and pens. Try to relax, or at least appear to be at ease. For the teacher, this is the difficult time. You want them to write. You can tell them to write. You can encourage them to write. But you can't write their papers for them.

You are now like a parent who is watching a child ride a bicycle for the first time. You want that child to go fast enough to maintain his or her balance, but not so fast that he or she can't stop the darned thing at a fence or at the curb of a busy street. But just remember — Somehow children do learn to ride bicycles, and they do learn to stop. Your students will write their Autobiographies, too.

By now all of your students should be writing. You've done it!

## Offer Immediate Approval!

After two or three minutes, you must start to walk quietly up and down the aisles, look over the shoulders of your students, and quickly glance at what they have written so far.

Because you do not want to interfere with the other students' thinking and writing, scan the first lines of each paper and tell the writer only loud enough for him or her to hear:

"Very good!"

"Good start!"

"Terrific beginning!"

Even though you don't really mean it, tell your students these wonderful things and sound as if you really do mean what you are saying, because *your students need your approval — IMMEDIATELY! RIGHT NOW!*

If you see a blank piece of paper that still has no writing on it, tell the

*You want them to write.*

*You can tell them to write.*

*You can encourage them to write.*

*But you can't write their papers for them.*

owner to write the first thing that pops into his or her mind. And say that you expect a full paragraph to be written by the time you walk by again. Then don't forget to return, read the lines, and congratulate the student on what he or she has written.

Your *IMMEDIATE APPROVAL* is vitally important to your students. It makes no difference if they are middle school, junior high, high school, college, or adult students, they need your positive comments — *RIGHT NOW!*

Before I knew better, I used to think the under-achieving or the learning-disabled students required immediate approval the most. Now I know the high-achieving students need it just as much — especially gifted students. I hope you will take this in the nature in which I mean it: When conducting creative courses, gifted students can sometimes be a real pain in the what-ever part of the anatomy you wish to designate. They *want so much to be right. They feel they have to be right.* And because of this, they often are afraid to take chances.

"Mr. Melton, I've just written my first sentence. Is it all right?" a student will ask nervously.

"It's very good!" I say.

"I've finished my first paragraph. Is it good enough?" another student has to know before continuing.

"Terrific!" I assure him or her.

And on and on.

Only after your students are truly confident that their teacher has approved of their work, will they relax and write freely on their own.

DO NOT neglect this important phase of *IMMEDIATE APPROVAL* at the beginning of *each and every assignment.* Your students not only <u>WANT</u> it, they <u>NEED</u> it!

## Let Your Students Solve Their Own Problems

Offering approval and solving problems for your students are two different things. While you are giving your approval and encouraging them to do their most creative work, it is important that you are not too eager to solve their problems for them.

Standing back is often difficult for teachers because we have been trained to "always be on tap" to answer questions and offer advice. Our students need us, but for what purpose do they need us? Do they need us to answer a question? Okay, we'll do that. Or are they trying to get us to do their thinking for them? We don't want to do that. We want them to think through their own work and learn to solve their own problems.

A long time ago, I became very good at saying, "What do **you** think?"

When a student asks, "Do you think this sentence is necessary?" I am quick to reply, "What do *you* think?"

Chances are, the student writer will answer, "I think it would be better if I wrote..." and then go on to express a wonderful, well-thought-out idea.

I love that! First, because I've gotten the student writer to think for himself or herself, which is my basic goal as a teacher. Second, I've gotten myself off the hook, because if I had made a suggestion that didn't help, the

*Your IMMEDIATE APPROVAL is vitally important to your students.*

*It makes no difference if they are middle school, junior high, high school, college, or adult students, they need your positive comments RIGHT NOW!*

*Offering approval and solving problems for your students are two different things.*

*Give your approval and encouragement, but don't be too eager to solve their problems for them.*

student is apt to eventually tell me that I was the one who loused up his or her story with my poor suggestion.

What's really fun about hitting a question back into the student's court is that, after they solve their own problems, they often thank me for my help.

## Watch the Time

*If you have anything to tell your students before the end of class, be sure to allow ample time to do so.*

If you have anything to tell your students before the end of class, be sure to allow ample time to do so. Never try to tell them anything after the bell has sounded and all of them are talking, laughing, and scrambling to get out of the classroom.

**Three minutes before the bell rings, tell them:**

> "I'm about to do a terrible thing to you. I'm going to stop you from writing."

**Then tell them to be sure to:**

1. Give your letter to their parents.

2. Complete their Autobiographies during the weekend.

3. Let them know that their Autobiographies are due to be handed in first thing *at the beginning of class on Monday*. There will be no time allowed for them to work further on their Autobiographies during Monday's class period.

**Then say to your class, "I'll see you Monday morning."**

If you have timed the end of the session just right, the bell will ring precisely at this point. The second it does, start to look very busy. Sorry, but you simply do not have time to talk with the one or two students who *always have additional questions*. Just tell them that all the information they need is on the ASSIGNMENT SHEET, then shoo them on their way.

## It Is Not an Oversight

You may have noticed that we assigned *AN AUTOBIOGRAPHY* without giving many formal instructions in writing. This is not an oversight. It was done on purpose.

Your students' Autobiographies will give you two important pieces of information:

1. Interesting facts about your students' lives; and

2. At what levels of skill your students now write.

## Wonderful Treasures!

Come Monday morning, you will have in your possession some wonderful treasures — the Autobiographies of your students. These are precious gifts. I hope you will regard these works as such and offer them the respect they deserve.

YOU'RE OFF TO A GOOD START!

# Be Prepared!  Be In Charge!

This is a very important session, because you are going to give a volume of vital information to your students during the hour.  So prepare yourself. And compose yourself.  You must appear relaxed, while making it evident that you are in charge.

## Worst Things, Best Things

Your students have written their Autobiographies and are ready to turn them in to you.

As a teacher, I always want to know what my students have experienced while they were writing, and I want to get them to open up and share those experiences in class.  So at the completion of each assignment, I take time (seven or eight minutes) to ask my students two questions.

*As a teacher, I always want to know what my students have experienced while they were writing, and I want them to open up and share those experiences in class.*

### Ask Question Number One:

While you were writing this assignment, what was the **worst thing** that happened to you?

I want answers from everyone, so starting at row one, I call on each person in class.  I love to hear their responses, and the students are interested, too, and listen carefully as the answers are given.  Their answers may include:

"The typewriter ribbon broke."

"The computer crashed and I had to rewrite my paper."

"We had company last night."

"I had to go to the store to get more paper."

"I had more thoughts than I could write down."

"I ran out of time."

"I had to stay up until after midnight to get finished."

Tell your students that theirs are the very same answers that professional writers give.

*...convincing your students that you have absolute faith in the fact that they do indeed have ideas is one of the most important factors in your success in teaching them how to improve their writing skills.*

Interestingly enough, we never hear from students the one answer that is the worst of the worst, and that is, "I didn't have any ideas."

Your students won't tell you they didn't have ideas because it wouldn't be true. The truth is, they are loaded with ideas — splendid ideas and wonderful ideas. And convincing your students that you have absolute faith in the fact that they do indeed have ideas is one of the most important factors in your success in teaching them how to improve their writing skills.

**Now ask them Question Number Two:**

What is the **best thing** that happened to you?

The answers will come readily:

"I finished."

"Good!" you say.

"I found I could get my thoughts down on paper."

"Wonderful!" you respond.

"I was surprised that I enjoyed it."

"Super!" you exclaim. "That's what we want!"

Covering the worst and the best things only takes a few minutes, but it is important time well spent. You will find your students' responses will change during the course. In time, their answers will be linked more closely to areas of composition and the aspects of writing skills:

"I wrote my ending three times because I wasn't satisfied with the first two."

"I had to condense some sections because they were too long."

"I had to add some sentences because the transitions between some paragraphs were too abrupt."

After everyone has answered with the worst and the best things, have them hand in their Autobiographies, and be sure to tell your students you are eager to read their papers.

Also tell them you will keep the Autobiographies until the end of the course. Then they will be returned.

NOTE: You keep the Autobiographies because you may at times want to review some of them. It's always interesting to compare and evaluate the outstanding improvements your students make throughout the course.

## Going Public

**Now is the time to announce the publishing surprise.**
**Tell your students:**

During this course, you will be writing a wide variety of assignments. The assignments you write will be read by many of your classmates, as well as other teachers and students throughout the school, not only during this school year, but in years to come.

At the end of this course, we will select your best papers, photocopy them, and bind them into a special book. We will present that book to the school library so your work can be seen and read by hundreds.

Great! You have told your students the good news and the bad news.

The good news is — What they write is going to be read by other people.

The bad news is — What they write is going to be read by other people.

In other words, you have complimented your students and threatened them at the same time.  Good for you!  You have just motivated and inspired your students to want to try do their best work, because what they produce is going to be published and seen by the public!

## Add to the Excitment With a Publishing Company

**Tell your students:**

To properly prepare your manuscripts for publication, we need to form a publishing company and give it a name.

Before I ask students to submit names for their publishing company, I always suggest to them that they offer names that are:

1.  Indigenous to the area, such as *Mountain View Publishing Company*; or *Sunflower Publishers;* or

2.  Related to school, such as *The Huskers' Publishing Company*, or *The Purple and Gold Publishing Company*; or

3.  Philosophical or goal-related names, such as *Dreamers United*; *Imaginations Unlimited*; or *Better Writing, Incorporated.*

However, when you ask for suggestions, you have to be willing to accept anything (well almost anything) as an absolutely wonderful idea, even though you think it is downright silly.  It is important for your students to understand that you will be open to their suggestions and will respond to them in a positive manner.

In a middle school in Kansas, I was president of the *Sock-It-To-Me Press*.  In the high school of a small town in Wyoming, I was the CEO of *The Herpes Publishing Company*.  When that name was suggested,  I was the only person in the room who didn't snicker.  Instead, I wrote the word on the board as if I thought *Herpes* was the Greek God of Literature.

Are there names I would not accept?  You betcha.  If someone offers a truly crude word, I have perfected a very effective facial expression that lets the person know I can't believe he or she would show such poor taste.  Then I ask for another suggestion.

**Now ask your students:**

What would you like to name your new publishing company?

As your students call out suggestions, you write the names on the chalk board.  After five names have been offered, let the class vote and declare the winner.  Leave the winning name on the board and erase all the others.

Congratulations!  Your class has formed a publishing company!

And by the way, you are the president of that publishing company.  Why are you automatically the president?  Because you didn't let your students vote on that.  My motto is — *Never let them vote on anything that you intend to decide.*

*...you have complimented your students and threatened them at the same time.*

## Keep On Moving!

**Write the following on the board:**

### THE BEST IDEAS
### COME FROM THE WORK,
### NOT FROM OUR HEADS.

This statement is so important to students that I always have them copy it and place the sheet where they can see it when they are writing. Tell them to carry it in their notebooks and keep it where they can refer to it, both at home and at school.

Explain to your students that it is a good statement for them to have before them because it is a true statement. Discuss with them that the best ideas often do come from the work. But rarely do these ideas appear within the first few sentences. Usually they don't come to light until the writer is further into the writing. Then absolutely wonderful ideas and turns of phrases start to snap, crackle, and pop, almost as if they have come from the paper itself, or the screen, or the air that surrounds the writer.

Remind your students that it is very important for the writer to physically place himself or herself in front of the paper or the computer screen, and *CONQUER THE POWER OF THE WHITE* by quickly writing the opening sentences, without caring if those sentences are carefully thought out or are structurally sound.

Assure your students that it is next to impossible for anyone to write three pages of text in which every single sentence and every single idea is so poor that nothing can be salvaged. If they write down enough words and enough thoughts, good ideas will burst forth. What is enough? Enough to let it happen, of course.

*...it is next to impossible for anyone to write three pages of text in which every single sentence and every single idea is so poor that nothing can be salvaged.*

## Good Input — Good Output

If you want to get good writing out of your students, then you need to put good information about writing into them.

**The following contains good, solid, important information about writing that your students need to hear and consider. So at this time, read this information aloud to them:**

### EVERYONE HAS STORIES TO WRITE

Human beings are amazing creatures! Every one of us has volumes of experiences from which we can draw when we tell and write stories. Many people take their own experiences for granted and don't think others would be interested in them. But the opposite is true. People are very interested, even fascinated, in the lives of others.

We enjoy hearing stories, reading books, going to plays, and seeing movies, because we hope to gain some insight, or at least a glimpse, of how other people live and react to situations that confront them. We are curious to know how people deal with others — the ones they like, the ones they dislike, the ones they admire, and the ones they fear. Through the media of literature and the performing arts, we have opportunities to vicariously live many lives, and we are introduced to thousands of people we otherwise might never meet.

All human beings have much in common with one another. We need food to eat, water to drink, and all of us have to go to the restroom.

*Human beings are amazing creatures! Every one of us has volumes of experiences from which we can draw when we tell and write stories.*

Yet, in thought or deed, we human beings are not simple creatures.  We are complex individuals who have egos and emotions with which we must contend. Beneath most of our Dr. Jekylls, there lurks a Mr. Hyde.  We can only hope that within every Mr. Hyde, at least a spark of Dr. Jekyll remains.  We do indeed have within us the capacity to muster courage of heroic proportions, but in some circumstances, we may react like cowards.

We have families.  Some of our families function as loving and caring units. Some families are dysfunctional in varying degrees and in a variety of ways. Some are torn apart by outside forces, while others self-destruct from within.

Most of us love our parents.  Some of our parents earn our love and our respect.  Others give us cause to distrust, dislike, and even despise them.  But within it all, most of us do have some sense of family or some idea of what a family should be or could be.  And we learn very early in life that even those people who care the most for each other do not always agree with one another, for every grouping of people is composed of individuals who have to make many adjustments in their daily give-and-take with others.

All communities have rules and rituals that their members are to honor and respect.  Those who break the rules are either punished, cast out, or done in. There are also universal laws that most cultures have in common.  Members may be encouraged to kill people of other tribes, either in acts of aggression or in defense of the group, but they are not supposed to kill members of their own tribe.

These things we have in common offer the writer a variety of opportunities to explore.  Readers are interested in the dynamics and nuances of the interactions of others.  And because readers share portions of common bonds, they can empathize with the characters and situations in books, stories, plays, and films.

Writers don't have to go to great lengths to expound on the rules and social orders of their own cultures, because their readers already know most of them. The majority of us know that we are not supposed to steal, or lie, or kill.  That saves the writer miles of typewriter ribbon and tons of paper.

The writer can also use physical things that all people experience.  For instance, I have never met anyone ten years of age or older who has never been burned.  The fact that everyone knows how even a minor burn feels is of enormous help to the writer.

Just think how difficult it would be for a writer, even with the skill of a Tolstoy, an Emerson, or a Cheever, to describe to persons who have never been burned, the exact sensation of pain that people feel when they burn a finger, or a hand, or a leg.  How many words, paragraphs, or pages would be required to describe that pain?  A lot!

However, because most readers know the pain of being burned, the author can tell them how the character stumbled and fell against the stove or into the fireplace.  The reader cringes as the character smells the burning flesh before he or she feels the agonizing pain.  Readers can smell the odor, too, and with instant recall, they feel the pain.  They squint their eyes and grit their teeth.

The author can increase the extent of the pain by increasing the intensity of the fire and by turning a first-degree burn into a second- or a third-degree burn.  Clothing catching fire strikes terror in the imaginations of readers.  And a burn to the character's face by hot grease or ignited gasoline sends shock waves of frantic horror.

It is doubtful that any writer can really describe the smell of cinnamon or the taste of apple pie to anyone who has never smelled cinnamon or tasted apple pie.  But let the author write "the spicy aroma of cinnamon," or "the sweet, tart taste of apple pie," and those readers who have experienced cinnamon will immediately smell it, and those who have eaten fresh apple pie will taste it.  These common experiences are extremely valuable assets that the writer can manipulate and use.

We human beings are also different from one another.  No two people are

*Most of us have families upon whom we depend. But we learn early in life that even those people who care the most for each other don't always agree with each other.*

*All of us,*
*including you and*
*including me,*
*have had interesting*
*experiences*
*in our lives*
*that provide us*
*with an abundance*
*of writing material.*

identical. Within each of our heads are two wet-cell computers called brains. From the beginning of time to the end of time, no two sets of brains have ever been identically formed. Unlike dry-cell computers that are mass produced by *IBM*, *Apple*, *Wang*, or any of the others, each human brain is individual and original. No two brains in human beings are programmed exactly alike either. Each brain program is unique.

Even those children who are related to each other and who live with the same family do not think exactly alike, nor do they perceive information alike or have the exact same interests or goals. When they write, they don't write like the others because each one sees and responds to human conditions differently — sometimes from slightly different viewpoints, sometimes in wild departures of perspective. These different viewpoints fascinate us. That's why we enjoy reading Stephen King, James Michener, Saul Bellow, Danielle Steele, Kurt Vonnegut, John Updike, Joyce Carol Oates, Lloyd Alexander, Sidney Sheldon, and a host of other notable authors.

We also are fascinated by the personalities of the day. That's why readers go to the newsstand by the millions and grab up copies of *Time*, *Newsweek*, and *People*. *The National Inquirer* is in supermarkets because "inquiring minds want to know" the latest dirt on a political figure, a movie star, or royalty. Admit it or not, human beings love gossip. We enjoy hearing the latest juicy tidbits about the outrageous goings-on of the rich and famous, as well as those of the infamous and controversial.

But whether rich or poor, plain or fancy, within every family there is a story which, if properly told, has the potential of becoming a published book. Everyone has had experiences that could be of interest to others. These are not second-rate stories in which only those personally involved have an interest. They often are first-rate dramas that contain powerful combinations of raw courage and family dynamics.

All of us, including you and including me, have had interesting experiences in our lives that provide us with an abundance of writing material. There isn't a ten-year-old child who hasn't had an experience that would not make a wonderful story. Twelve-year-olds are loaded with experiences. And as for teenagers and adults, they have a cornucopia of experiential events, encounters, and ideas about which they may choose to write and share with people.

Within each person's life there are valuable experiences from which he or she can draw in creating stories that other people would love to read.

## The Six Hurdles

Note: In a previous chapter, I listed for you the Six Hurdles that discourage people from writing. It is now the time to present a simpler version of these Six Hurdles to your students.

**Look directly at your students and tell them:**

There are six reasons why you may be discouraged from writing.

**Then go to the board, list those reasons, and read them aloud:**

  1. NO GUARANTEED READERS

  2. NO DEADLINES

  3. NO EDITORS

  4. DON'T KNOW HOW TO EDIT YOUR OWN WORK

  5. DON'T WRITE OFTEN ENOUGH

  6. NO REGARD FOR YOUR READERS

## Let's Remove Every "*No*" and "*Don't*"

**Now, one at a time, *ERASE* the first word in each item on the list.**

**As you progress down the list, give your students the explanation that follows each item:**

**1. NO GUARANTEED READERS —**

**Tell your students:**

During this course, you will be given **guaranteed readers**.  At least four other students will read your manuscripts, and I will read them, too.  So you will have at least five readers for every paper you write.

**2. NO DEADLINES —**

**Tell your students:**

You will be given a **deadline** for each and every assignment.  You must meet those deadlines to insure that others can read your papers and help you improve them.  You are responsible for finishing your paper on time and turning it in on time.  If you are ill the day of the deadline, make sure someone brings your paper to me before class.  That's absolutely essential!

**3. NO EDITORS —**

**Tell your students:**

You will have **editors** — five of them.  Each one of you will be assigned another student to be your Continuing Editor.  During the entire course, your Continuing Editor will read all of your manuscripts and assist you in editing these papers. You will be assigned as a Continuing Editor for another student's work.

Then, each of you will have at least three other student editors who will review and edit your work.

I will be your fifth editor because I will read and edit all your manuscripts.

**4. DON'T KNOW HOW TO EDIT YOUR OWN WORK —**

**Tell your students:**

You will soon know **how to edit your own work**, because you will learn methods by which you can edit and improve your own manuscript.

**5. DON'T WRITE OFTEN ENOUGH —**

**Tell your students:**

I assure you, you will **write enough**.  During this course you will write twelve manuscripts, which will mean that you will be writing more than enough, and probably more than you ever have before.

**6. NO REGARD FOR YOUR READERS —**

**Tell your students:**

Before you begin each assignment, you will develop a high **regard for your readers** when you select a "specific" reading audience for that particular manuscript.  A "general" reading audience will not be acceptable because it is not specific enough.

A fifty-two-year-old construction worker in Los Angeles, California, will have very different interests and questions than would a fourteen-year-old boy who is in the seventh grade, or a forty-year-old woman who is president of a large corporation in New

*During this course, your students will be given Readers, Deadlines, and Editors. Your students will learn how to edit. They will write a lot. And they will gain a high regard for their readers.*

*Once your students have selected an audience, they can envision their readers as real people. Then they can write directly to those real people.*

York City, or a twenty-year-old college student in Sao Paulo, Brazil.

Your choice of audience must be very specific — sixteen-year-old girls, six-year-old children, middle school gifted students, high school teen-age dropouts, parents of troubled teenagers, or mid-western adult farmers, etc. Once you have selected your audience, you can envision your readers as real people. Now you can write your paper to those real people. Once you regard your readers as people, your writing will have better direction and purpose. Your writing will also become easier and more meaningful.

Within days you are going to be writing better than you ever have before. The fine quality of your writing will surprise some of your classmates. You are going to be thrilled and excited by the fine quality of writing your classmates produce. You may also be surprised by the improved quality of your own work.

**Then be sure you emphasize again:**

When we finish this course, we are going to publish a book that will contain the best pieces of writing from this class. Each of you will have at least one piece included. That book will be presented to our school library.

---

Printed on Page 45

## ASSIGNMENT NO. 2 — A PROFILE OF A PERSON WHO MOST INFLUENCED YOUR LIFE IN A POSITIVE WAY OR WAYS

**Now hand out copies of:**
**ASSIGNMENT SHEET NO. 2 — A PROFILE OF A PERSON WHO MOST INFLUENCED YOUR LIFE IN A POSITIVE WAY OR WAYS.**
**Read the Assignment Sheet aloud and explain the information.**

Give your students the date of the deadline, and have them write it on their copies.

Three days should be plenty of time on this assignment. It requires no research. The students already know the information they will need. All they have to do is write.

If you like, you may allow time during class on the next day for them to work on the assignment. But remember, that is writing time, not discussing time. Do not discuss their writing with them until it is completed.

## The Lengths of the Assignments Are Engraved in Stone

**Tell your students, the length of each writing assignment is exact:**
250 words means 250 words.
750 words means 750 words.
1,000 words means 1,000 words.

Are exceptions allowed? Yes. Students are allowed to have *five percent over* or *five percent under* the specified number of words. On 750 words, they may turn in a paper that contains 712 words or 788 words. But those are the limits.

# A Profile of a Person Who Most Influenced Your Life In a Positive Way or Ways

Deadline: _____

Number of Words: 1000

Number of Copies: 2
(One for teacher and one for others to edit)

---

**pro·file** (prō′īl′), *n.* an informal biographical sketch.

**in·flu·ence** (ĭn′flōō-ens), *n., v., —n.* 1. the capacity or power of persons or things to produce effects on others by intangible or indirect means.

**pos·i·tive** (pŏz′ĭ-tĭv), *adj.* 1. confident in opinion or assertion; sure. 15. measured or proceeding in a direction assumed as beneficial, progressive, or auspicious: *a positive trend.*

— Random House Webster's College Dictionary

---

During the course of our lives, all of us have had people who have offered us a special kindness or who have helped us in some positive way or ways.

Select such a person in your life. That person may be a relative, a friend, or an acquaintance.

Write a profile of the person you select.

In your manuscript:

- Describe the person physically;

- Tell how the person moves and talks;

- Make the person come alive to the reader;

- Tell how that person helped you and/or taught you some thing or things that made an improvement in your life.

Write your manuscript in a sequence that is interesting, and then give your paper an interesting title.

**Figuring five percent plus or minus:**

5% of 250 words = 12 1/2 words.

5% of 500 words = 25 words.

5% of 1,000 words = 50 words.

**It is easy to count the number of words a manuscript contains:**

1. Count the number of words in ten lines.

2. Divide the total number of words in those ten lines by ten, which will equal the average number of words per line.

3. Now count the number of lines on each page.

4. Then multiply the number of lines by the average number of words per line, which will give the total number of words per page.

5. If one page has 250 words, which is average for double-spaced, typed pages, you will need three pages to complete a 750-word assignment.

*Do long words count the same as short words?*

*Yes! Supercalifragilistic-expialidocious counts as one word, but so do I, a, it, me, and so on.*

"Do long words count the same as short words?" students will ask.

"Yes!" you answer. "*Supercalifragilisticexpialidocious* counts as one word, but so do *I*, *a*, *it*, *me*, and so on."

As their teacher, you must not waiver from the strict rules you have given to your students. Let your students know in no uncertain terms that the rules are typed on their assignment sheets as firmly as if they had been carved in tablets of stone.

## How To Develop Manuscripts

**Tell your students the three stages in the development of a manuscript:**

1. ROUGH DRAFT

   The writer composes a first draft all the way through, without reading, rereading, or editing along the way. The main purpose of the rough is to get the ideas on paper. Spelling and punctuation are not important at this point.

2. IMPROVED VERSION

   After the rough is finished (and not until it is finished), the writer reads and rereads the work, starts the editing, corrects spelling and punctuation, and rewrites and improves the work.

   Note: There is good reason for not editing or rewriting sections of a draft until that draft is completed. Editing calls the academic brain into action. And we don't want to put the academic brain in control during the creative writing process.

3. COMPLETED MANUSCRIPT

   Once the writer is satisfied with the editing and the improvements of the work, and all spelling and punctuation is as near perfect as the writer can make it, bring the manuscript to class on the day of the deadline.

**Now tell your students:**

Open your notebooks to a clean sheet of paper, select the audience to whom you wish to write, and then immediately—
***CONQUER THE POWER OF THE WHITE!***
Start writing!
No, you do not have to worry about spelling on the first rough.

You must make sure that your students have at least twenty minutes of uninterrupted time to write.

## A Wonderful Assignment

ASSIGNMENT NO. 2 — A PROFILE OF A PERSON WHO MOST INFLUENCED YOUR LIFE IN A POSITIVE WAY OR WAYS, is a wonderful assignment for your students and for you.

Don't tell your students, but this assignment is really an extension of the Autobiographies they have just handed in to you. Once you read your students' Autobiographies, you are going to know a lot about each person in your class. Now, through their writings about the influential people they admire, you will learn even more about your students.

The influential people — relatives, friends, teachers, employers, neighbors, and so on — are extremely important to the students. Be grateful that they have chosen to share with you another private and meaningful part of their lives.

*...through your students' writings about the influential people they admire, you will learn even more about your students.*

## Why "Positive Ways" Only?

I always insist upon having students write about people who have affected their lives *only in positive ways*, because I long ago learned my lesson about *negative ways*.

The first time I made ASSIGNMENT NO. 2 was in a class of adults, and I didn't specify *positive ways*. I just said, "The person who most influenced your life."

The assignment was to consist of 1,250 words, which was five typewritten pages, double-spaced. But from one of the women in the class, I received a thirty-six-page document about her ex-husband, in which she really "vented her spleen." She told more intimate details about their marriage and their divorce than I ever would want to know.

Her catharsis on paper made me wonder if people can write longer papers when they are angry and out for revenge. At any rate, I never wanted to chance it again, so I added *positive ways* to the directions. I'm glad I did. I think you will be, too.

## Back to the Class

Now look around the room. If all your students are now writing, you can be satisfied that you have done your job well, and you can begin to walk around the room, look over their shoulders, say encouraging things to them, and give your IMMEDIATE APPROVAL to them.

About two minutes before the bell rings, stop everyone from writing. Tell them they will need to get a three-ring, loose-leaf notebook to hold their assignment sheets, their notes, and their working drafts and edited manuscripts.

The bell rings.  Class dismissed.

## Do Not Discuss the Assignment Or Offer Suggestions

Don't let your students linger and attempt to involve you in discussions about their assignments.  Act absolutely confident that they can solve their own problems.

## How To Read Your Students' Autobiographies

*When I read my students' Autobiographies, I am reminded that in my class there are living, breathing human beings who expect and deserve my very best.*

I never attempt to read my students' Autobiographies when I am tired or feel rushed.  I will schedule a time when I am relaxed and can really concentrate.  I always look intently at the photograph of the student on the cover and, as I read, I make certain that I connect the written information with his or her face.

The Autobiographies always provide a variety of experiences.  I know during the course of reading that I will sometimes be moved to laughter and at other times to tears.  I often gain a true admiration for the students, because so many of them have survived extraordinary events and experiences in their lives.  They have endured pain and sorrow, and they have overcome great obstacles.  And as they write about themselves, a little miracle often happens or a channel seems to open, and they also reveal their hopes and their dreams.  I always think it is such a privilege to read what they have willingly offered to share with me.

At this point I am always reminded that my classroom consists of more than just warm bodies.  In my class there are living, breathing human beings who deserve and have the right to expect me to offer them my very best as a teacher and as a person.

I always make notes as I read, and I list at least one thing I find to be most interesting in each student's autobiography.  It is so important for students to know that I have indeed read their papers.  So I make a point of quietly thanking each student and telling that person how much I appreciate what he or she has chosen to share with me.

I hope you will do the same.

# Writing Is Writing!

*Just as athletes need to routinely exercise their muscles, writers must routinely exercise the writing and thinking areas of their brains.*

While your students are working on their first two or three assignments, don't be surprised if they are a little grouchy and out of sorts when they come to class. It's a commitment for them to explore deep within their minds, seek out things to write, and find the best way to express their thoughts, especially if they are not used to writing every day. When one doesn't write often enough, the writing areas of the brain are bound to be a little rusty and out of shape. Just as athletes need to routinely exercise their muscles, writers must routinely exercise the writing and thinking areas of their brains.

But as we have discussed, writing is good for people, and thinking is good for them, too. So don't let your students bring their problems to you for you to solve. Exude utmost confidence in their abilities to think through their own problems and come up with appropriate answers.

## Don't Tell It!
## Always Write It First!

I never listen to a student tell me about what he or she is going to write. It's not that I'm not interested because, in truth, I am very interested. It's simply that I don't think it's a good idea for a writer to tell anyone what he or she is going to write.

I never tell anyone a story or a section that I'm about to write. I learned long ago that once I tell it aloud, it is exceedingly difficult for me to write it. The spoken story is very different from a written text. The forms are different. The thought patterns are different. And the emphasis on tonality changes. You want your students to tell their stories in the written form, not in the spoken form.

Today, if you wish, give your students the full hour to write about their influential persons. If your students are writing, it will be a productive hour. This also offers you an hour to read some of their Autobiographies.

## "Magic Moments"

Most successful writers talk about the *"magic moments"* that occur as they work — those moments when everything in the writing starts to take on a life of its own. Ideas seem to leap from the page of paper or out of the computer screen. Sentences begin to flow like ribbons. Paragraphs seem to compose themselves. These moments are magical indeed! At such times, gamblers say they are "on a roll," with everything coming up sevens and elevens. Joggers say that when they are running, they suddenly reach a "high" — a state of euphoria, and they feel they could run forever.

The same thing happens in writing. When writers suddenly reach such a "high," they no longer feel they are doing the writing at all, but have then become mediums for an outside or an inside force that dictates the words and thoughts to them. It's an exhilarating experience! Writers speak of their "magic moments" with reverence and wish they would happen more often.

These *"magic moments"* rarely occur while writing the first sentence or paragraph, or even during the first ten minutes of writing. That's why it is important for assignments to be lengthy enough to allow the students to write long enough and often enough for their *"magic moments"* to occur.

> *"Magic Moments" are those times when everything in the writing starts to take on a life of its own. Sentences and paragraphs seem to compose themselves. When that happens, these moments are magical indeed!*

## How Long Is Long Enough?

Every once in a while, I have teachers tell me, "You'll be happy to know, I have my students write every day."

"How long do you have them write?" l ask.

"About ten minutes."

"Ten minutes!" I want to respond in exclamation!!! "That doesn't make me happy at all! I do my worst writing during the first ten minutes! It takes me that long to switch brains and really get started! Poor kids! Every day they have only ten-minute warm-ups to write their worst work! No wonder so many people wind up thinking they can't write well!"

So how long is long enough? In class, a minimum of twenty minutes. Forty-five minutes is even better. You always want to give students enough time to switch to their creative brains. When they are at home, they can write for as long as they want.

## How Often Is Often Enough?

EVERY DAY! Your students should be absorbed in the written word in some manner every day. We want them either to write every day or be involved with the editing process every day. The more involved they become in writing and editing, the better are their chances of experiencing those "magic moments" in their work or learning from the writings of their classmates.

## How About *"Group Brainstorming?"*

Do you know what a camel is? It's a horse put together by a committee.

When it comes to creative writing, I have a thorough dislike for *group brainstorming* and committee decisions. *Group brainstorming* and *group webbing* can be fun games for groups. But for the most part, writing is **not** a group activity.

Writing is *an individual process in THINKING*. Ideas come forth from the individual writer's brain. To seek out those ideas, the individual writer needs the opportunity to search the depths of his or her own brain in order to discover his or her own thoughts, instead of being influenced by others.

The best writing comes from a one-on-one confrontation between the academic brain and the creative brain, which are housed inside the same head. So it is imperative that you allow your writers to engage in *individualized THINKING* within their own brains.

Give your students the assignment without unnecessary chitchat and explanations, and without having to hear the suggestions and opinions of others in the class. Let each student explore his or her own ideas. Let their academic brains debate with their creative brains on a one-on-one basis. That's brainstorming at its very best, and it's called *individualized brainstorming!* Save the group kind of brainstorming for deciding what color to paint the classroom walls and which way to arrange the desks.

As their teacher, you should concentrate your efforts toward encouraging your students to *THINK* and *CREATE* independently of you and everyone else in the room. The success of this course is not measured by how similar are all the writings of twenty or thirty students. The ultimate success is achieved when all the manuscripts are very different from all the others. Each and every work should be individual and unique.

*The best writing comes from a one-on-one confrontation between the academic brain and the creative brain, which are housed inside the same head.*

## Pre-Writing Phase — Writing Phase

Some people think of the *pre-writing phase* as the preliminary work rituals writers must go through just before they start to write, such as making lists and outlines, the webbing of ideas, and the sharpening of twelve pencils.

I view *pre-writing* in a much broader sense than that. I think *pre-writing* is anything and everything one sees and hears, reads and feels, and thinks and experiences from the moment of one's birth to the moment the writer starts to write an article, a paper, a letter, a book, a script, or whatever. In essence, writers constantly live their lives in a *pre-writing phase* until they start to write. Then, when they write, they will be in the *writing phase*.

When they are in the *writing phase*, the ideas will come. And as writers begin work on a piece of writing, they have their lifetime of experiences, thoughts, emotions, and information from which they may bring forth memories and ideas.

Three o. the assignments in this course: *An Autobiography; A Profile of a Person Who Most Influenced Your Life in a Positive Way or Ways; and A Personal Remembrance,* will urge your students to consider and value the lifetimes of *pre-writing* experiences they have acquired and stored.

## In Sequence — Out of Sequence

Some writers always start by writing the very first sentence of a story, an article, or a book. Both Richard Rhodes and Robert Burch told me that until they are completely pleased with the first paragraph in a manuscript, they won't start the second one. I agree that the first paragraph of a book or a piece of writing is very important for capturing the interest of the reader. But I never have thought the reader cared, or even considered, if the first

*I see the construction of a written work as a patchwork of sentences, and paragraphs, and ideas that can be arranged and sewn together to form an overall quilt.*

paragraph was the first one written or the last one written, or if it was created somewhere in-between.

Alberta Wilson Constant, the author of the *Miller Girl* series of books, told me she always wrote the last chapter of a book first. She said if she wasn't pleased with the last chapter, she didn't intend to waste her time in writing all the others.

In a strange way, Ms. Constant's approach makes sense to me, but I don't think I could compose a book in that manner. I think I'm more of a middle-man. I usually start somewhere in the middle of the manuscript and work my way toward the front or the back, as the mood strikes me or the writing guides me. I have found there are certain advantages to my hop, skip, and jump method, especially when a mystery is involved in the story. When I know some of the events that occur in later scenes, it helps me place proper clues in earlier sections.

I see the construction of a written work as a patchwork of sentences, and paragraphs, and ideas. Once the individual parts are completed, then they can be arranged and sewn together with transitional threads to form the finished product, much like my grandmother used to compose and stitch when she made her beautiful quilts.

If your students start by first writing the middle of their papers, or even the endings, leave them alone, and they will come home, developing their beginnings behind them.

## There Is No Such Thing As *Writer's Block!*

There is procrastination. There is laziness. There is lack of discipline. But there is no such thing as *writer's block!*

I think *writer's block* is a term that was made up by nonwriters, because full-time professional writers know they can't afford to have *writer's block*.

Let me ask you something. As a professional teacher, do you ever get *teacher's block?* If you get *teacher's block*, what do you do about it? Do you walk into the principal's office and say, "Sorry, I can't teach today because I have *teacher's block*."

You know better than to try that, don't you? So what do you do when you think you have *teacher's block*? You teach! Right? Right!

When professional writers get what's been called *writer's block*, what do they do? They write! They know that editors are no more interested in *writer's blocks* than principals are in *teacher's blocks*.

Professional writers also know that if they place enough words on paper, something positive will eventually happen. A terrific idea will suddenly ignite and form a good paragraph, and the manuscript will be off and running.

So you see, I don't allow any of my students to have *writer's block*.

I once had a twelve-year-old student say, "Mr. Melton, I can't write this morning because I have *writer's block*."

"Nonsense!" I replied. "You're not allowed to have *writer's block* until you've had at least two books published."

"Oh, I didn't know that," the girl said seriously, and she returned to her desk and started writing.

Don't allow your students to even think about *writer's block*. Don't talk about it or discuss it, or even consider it. If you start to think about it — forget it! If a student mentions *writer's block*, tell him or her it's in the same category as Santa Claus, the Easter Bunny, and the Tooth Fairy.

There are *no blocked writers* allowed in this course!

## Expect the Unexpected

I make this promise to you — You will **not** be able to predict which of your students will create the best writing. The best papers may not come from your top-notch scholars. They may come from the very students whom you least expect. This happens all the time. The best writing may come from a student who has previously had difficulties in making passing grades, or from that drifter who, up to now, has sat in class, seemingly disinterested in anything and everything, or from that wild hare trouble-maker who looks and acts like the last rider from Hell's Angels.

However, up to now, most of your students have had no idea that their thoughts or ideas can be placed on paper in interesting and even dramatic ways. Most of them do not know, especially the disinterested students, what happens when they begin the intimate activity of personally composing a piece of writing. Most never have experienced having their imaginations suddenly catch fire. Most don't realize that they can create a composition of outstanding brilliance.

Some students have so much bottled up inside themselves that once they make the writing connection, it is as if the flood gates are thrown open to release tidal waves of thoughts and ideas. Then they surprise everyone, including the teacher and certainly themselves, by making amazing improvements in their writing skills.

I love to discover these students in my workshops! I love to have students who are considered losers, suddenly write a paper that is of such fine quality, it knocks everyone on their ears.

When this occurs, three things happen:

1. Teachers and parents begin to consider these students with higher regard;

2. The students' classmates begin to respond to and treat them with new respect; and

3. The self-esteems of the students receive a healthy boost.
   It is absolutely thrilling to observe the growth in each student's awareness of his or her own self-worth.

During this course, one of your most unlikely students is liable to write a paper that will tingle your senses and blow your mind!

SO — EXPECT THE UNEXPECTED!

*I make this promise to you — You will **not** be able to predict which of your students will create the best writing.*

# The Great Cover-up!

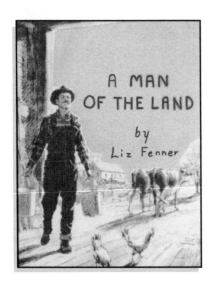

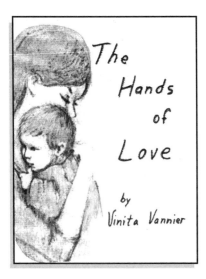

The day after your students start preparing ASSIGNMENT NO. 2 — A PROFILE OF A PERSON WHO MOST INFLUENCED YOUR LIFE IN A POSITIVE WAY OR WAYS, is a good time for you to give their brains another jolt of surprise.

## The Great Cover-Up!

One of the things that really bothered me about teaching a writing course was knowing that when the manuscripts were turned in, I was going to have to face all those plain, typed pages. Other than with the differences in titles and names of the authors, I knew all the title pages were destined to look alike. How boring!

Okay, I know I'm a visual person. I admit it. I like color and design. I enjoy creative displays of imagination. I never have wanted to shuffle through look-alike manuscripts and try to choose the one I might want to read first, or second, or third, and so on. And I didn't intend to do that. In order to make my choices more interesting, I decided I would have my students compete for my attention by designing attractive covers for each of their assignments.

The first group who designed covers were participants in one of my professional writing courses. All of them were adults. There was a doctor, a lawyer, a nurse, a nutritionist, a mortician, a space scientist, a magazine writer, a CEO of a sizable company, and among them were an elementary school teacher and a secondary teacher.

When I made the cover assignment, those persons who probably hadn't touched a crayon since they were in the fifth grade, sat there in stone silence and looked at me in disbelief. But not the elementary teacher. She giggled and said aloud, "This is going to be fun!" Then the secondary teacher smiled in agreement.

The rest of the class offered no discernible expressions of acceptance, nor was there any display of open rebellion. At least no tomatoes or rocks were thrown at me. I considered that to be a favorable sign.

I had no idea what a commotion these covers were going to cause. On the day the participants brought their covers to class, I displayed them on the trays beneath the chalkboards. When we saw how attractive and clever they were, many of us gasped, and the room was filled with their "oohs" and "aahs." Most of the covers were quite attractive and interesting, but some of them were very absolutely sensational.

For the next fifteen minutes, the cover designs were the topic of discussion. Everyone in class stood up and walked to the front of the room for a closer look. It was really exciting!

During the next weeks, the displays of covers became even more exciting, because the covers got progressively better and better. The participants became very competitive designers. All wanted to create the most attractive, or the most powerful, or the most beautiful, or the cleverest, or the funniest cover in class. And every time the assignments were brought in, all traffic stopped until all the covers were displayed and enjoyed.

## Properly Packaged and Brilliantly Presented!

No matter what their ages, it is a wonderful feeling writers have when they see their pages of writing appear in neat, typed rows, with correct spellings, perfect punctuations, and even margins of space on each side. But when they also see their manuscripts, handsomely enclosed in creatively designed, properly packaged covers — Wow! Then their written pages look important and cared for. It is an idea brilliantly presented. Oh, what it does for the pride and self-esteem of the writers!

I've taught this writing course to groups of professional people, to teachers, to college students, to high school students, and to middle school students, and their reactions to the covers are always the same. The covers are always one of the hits of the course. Students thoroughly enjoy creating them and seeing those created by their classmates. Your students are going to have a wonderful time, too. And you are going to love it!

So remember — the day after the second assignment is begun is the time to inform your students about the "great cover-up."

**Explain the following to your students:**

I am going to read all of your manuscripts very carefully, which means I will have a lot of reading to do.

Although I want to give each and every one of your papers my very best, I know my energy will be higher and my concentration will be better on the first papers I read. Those students whose papers I read first will, in all probability, get better responses from me.

But I have discovered a fair method by which I select the papers I will read first. I select those papers in the same way I select magazines from a counter or books from a shelf, and that is by first looking at their covers. So you should design a cover for your manuscript that grabs my attention, because I will pick the manuscript that has the most interesting cover and read it first. Then I will look at the next most interesting cover.

Therefore, if you want your manuscript to be among the first read, you should create a terrific cover!

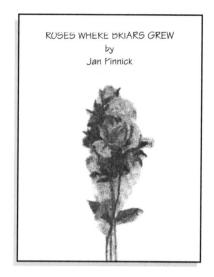

Printed on Page 57

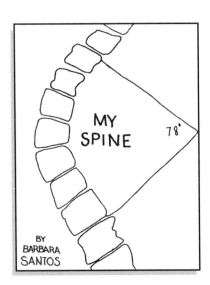

**Now pass out copies of THE GREAT COVER-UP! SHEET.**
As students look at the sheet, read the information aloud to them.

## Great Covers Attract More Readers

**Tell your students:**

Good visual presentations are very important toward encouraging people to read pieces of writing. That is why there are exciting pictures and splashy headlines on the front covers of magazines and newspapers, book jackets, movie billboards, CD containers, and advertisements of all kinds.

A good cover may be *bright* and *clever*, or *bold* and *powerful*, or *quiet* and *sensitive*, or *light* and *witty*, or even *outrageously funny*. But most importantly, the cover design should be *in perfect harmony with the personality and the content of the written work it holds inside*.

## Be Prepared for Some Moans and Groans

"But I can't draw a straight line!" someone is bound to say. *(I wish whoever coined that phrase had been boiled in axel grease!)*

"I didn't say you had to draw it," you respond. "I said create it. You may use pictures from magazines or newspapers as illustrations if you like."

"Does it have to be in color?"

"No, it may be black and white."

"Will anyone else see it besides you?"

"Your Continuing Editor and your classmates will see it. Other teachers and students are going to see it, too." *(That really adds pressure.)*

"You mean *everyone* in school might see it?" they ask in alarm.

"Yes, so you want to do a good job."

"Do we have to make two covers, one for each copy?"

"No. Make one cover, then photocopy it for the second copy."

"But, who gets the original?"

"I do!" you reply. "I'm the president of your publishing company."

If your students ask why they are expected to design covers for a writing course, you might explain to them that you are not teaching just a **WRITING COURSE;** it is also a **THINKING COURSE**. You are assigning them to *think*, *analyze*, and *expand* what they have written into a *visual presentation*.

Then tell your students you are looking forward to seeing the covers they will design for their final manuscripts.

## Plastic Protectors

Some of your students may want to protect the covers they design. You might suggest having them get plastic, slide-lock report protectors. These are inexpensive and they can be reused.

The clear plastic ones are best. They allow the students' covers to be seen. And the plastic bar on the left-hand side holds all the pages and the covers securely together.

# THE GREAT COVER-UP!

Design an interesting cover for your manuscript.
A good cover is composed of three elements:

1. Title
2. Name of Author
3. An Interesting Illustration

## Examples:

## But your cover will be even better!

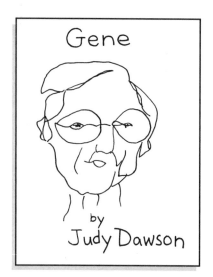

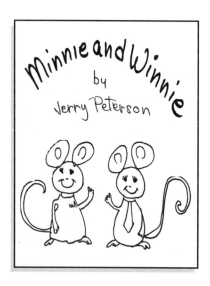

## Pressure! Pressure! Pressure!

Your students probably will grouse about the pressure of deadlines and that you are not allowing them enough time to complete their work. Let such complaints fall on deaf ears.

The pressure of deadlines is an asset *for* writers and *for* cover designers. It doesn't work against them. Pressure makes them switch brains, change gears, and bolt into action, or at least keep moving forward.

Remember, creative brains don't need a lot of time.

At this point, you want your students to conclude an important thing about you —

They don't know what you're going to do next.

You also want them to realize an important thing about the course —

It is unlike any course they have ever taken.

## An Extra Plus!

Now that you have told your students to create covers, they will start *THINKING* even more and using their brains in new and exciting ways. Not only will they be thinking about what their papers will say in words; they will consider what their papers are going to look like. That is a big plus! As they become interested in designing attractive, attention-getting covers, they will start looking at magazine covers and book jackets more carefully than ever before.

"What is good about that cover?" they will analyze.

"Why does that one grab my attention?" they'll consider.

"I like those colors!" they will declare.

"My cover needs to look more powerful," they will determine.

Or they will wisely conclude —

"My cover has to be *beautiful*, or *elegant*, or *bright*, or *vivid*, or *sensitive*, or *as funny as all get out*."

Your students will watch television more critically, too. They will pay more attention to the advertisements and the images that flash before their eyes. They now are in search of visual ideas that will reach out and grab the attention of their viewers. That is called research and new awareness. Students are sure to want to create covers that will make their classmates sit up and take notice. They definitely will want their teacher to be pleased with their covers.

You should be applauded for what you have done for your students. You have been successful in awakening their interests in the exciting worlds of print and visual media. You have motivated them to observe and analyze written and visual messages. You have encouraged them to spend additional time outside the classroom in researching and exploring written and visual presentations.

The truth is — Learning does not begin or end at the sound of the bell. With each and every assignment, you will send your students forth to learn far more than you ever could teach them in class.

**NOW — WE COME TO MY FAVORITE PART!**

# Happy Harvest!

## The Big Day Arrives

Today, your students bring in two copies of their finished manuscripts of — A PROFILE OF A PERSON WHO MOST INFLUENCED YOUR LIFE IN A POSITIVE WAY OR WAYS.

**Before the copies are handed in, take time to ask each and every student the *Worst* and the *Best things*, by saying:**

While you were preparing your assignment, what is the *worst thing* that happened to you?

Take enough time for every student to give a reply to both questions, but don't let the answers drag on for any longer than seven or eight minutes.

If one of the students tells you the *worst thing* was that he or she didn't get finished, tell him or her that was indeed the *worst thing* that could have happened, because it means that his or her editor will not be able to read and edit the manuscript.

You want to publicly inform your students that when a manuscript is not completed on time, everyone in class loses something. The student writer loses immediate acceptance and respect as a conscientious participant in the course. The student editors and the teacher lose the opportunity to read and enjoy the manuscript within the time scheduled.

You want to make the student aware that he or she not only failed in the responsibility to complete his or her own work, but he or she also failed a responsibility to other students in the class. You want to be firm in making these points clear, so the negligent student comprehends the seriousness of what he or she has done, but not be so harsh that the embarrassed student bursts into tears or commits hari-kari in front of your desk. You know what I mean.

**Next, ask each and every student:**

While you were preparing your assignment, what was the *best thing* that happened to you?

*Deadlines are important — students must accept the responsibility of completing their work on time.*

The students' answers will vary.

"I finished it!" may signify a sense of accomplishment.

"My mother liked it," can indicate that the writer felt a need to have the work favorably accepted by a reader.

Both are good answers, but when a student says —

"*I* like what I've written!" that answer may be the best one yet.

## Let the Excitement Begin!

Instruct your students to, one at a time, bring the original copy of their manuscript to the front of the class, hold it up so everyone can see the cover, tell the class the title, and then hand the manuscript to you.

If your room has a chalk tray under the chalkboard, stand the papers on the tray for everyone to see.

This first time, some of the covers may not look like they are out of a New York advertising agency or the Pratt Art Institute. It will be obvious that some students didn't spend a lot of time on their cover designs or give them very much thought. But there will be other covers that will be absolute knock-outs. Those knock-outs will garner sounds of approval and admiration. One or two covers may be so sensational, the class will even applaud.

Your students are not dummies. They will quickly realize that approval and enthusiastic applause are far preferable to tightened frowns and silent stares that poorer quality covers receive. But be assured, the covers your students design for subsequent papers will be much better, because they will be more thoughtful and more creative. Not only are their cover designs going to improve; so will their writing. You'll see.

## Time To Assign Continuing Editors

It is now time to assign Continuing Editors for each writer. Except for you, a writer's Continuing Editor is the first person to be allowed to read the writer's manuscript.

**Assigning the Continuing Editor for each writer is easy**.

**Step One:**

Have your students take the second copy of their manuscripts and line up in two rows — Row A and Row B — and face each other. If anyone is facing a best friend, have one of those students switch places with someone else. Best friends usually are not the best editors for each other.

The people in Row A are Writers.

The people in Row B are Continuing Editors.

Writers in Row A hand the copy of their manuscripts to their Continuing Editors who are in Row B.

**Step Two:**

Next have everyone in Row A trade places with the person standing to their right, with the person farthest to the right moving down to the left-hand end of the line. Now every person in Row A is facing a different person in Row B, who should also not be a best friend.

Now the people in Row A are Continuing Editors.

*Your students are not dummies. They will quickly realize that approval and enthusiastic applause are far preferable to tightened frowns and silent stares.*

The people in Row B are the Writers.

Each writer in Row B hands his or her manuscript to the person facing him or her in Row A, who is now that writer's Continuing Editor.

At this point, every writer has a Continuing Editor. And every Continuing Editor has a writer. To avoid future confusion, quickly make a list of who is what for whom.

In two or three minutes, the process is completed.

Now have your students put their papers away and clear their desks.

*All of your writers now have Continuing Editors, and all of your Continuing Editors have writers!*

## The Function of an Editor

**Write the following statement on the chalkboard and read it aloud:**

*The function of an Editor is to improve the work.*
*It is not to intimidate the writer and destroy his or her confidence.*

**Now pass out copies of the:**
    **PROFESSIONAL EDITORIAL INFORMATION SHEET.**
**Read the information aloud and explain all the editorial markings.**

## But Where Should They Paragraph?

Even those students who write well may have problems in knowing when to paragraph. I tell them three simple rules for paragraphing:

**Rule One:**
**Each time you change major subjects, paragraph.**

**Rule Two:**
**Each time a character or a different character speaks, paragraph.**

"Little pig, little pig, let me come in," said the big bad wolf.

"Not by the hair of my chinny-chin-chin," replied the first little pig.

"Then I'll huff and I'll puff, and I'll blow your house in!" the wolf howled.

**Rule Three:**
**Anytime you have more than six typewritten lines, paragraph.**
**You'll be right more times than you'll be wrong.**

I realize this last suggestion may make the some English teachers' hair stand on end and cause William Faulkner to turn over in his grave, but today we are used to reading *Time* magazine and newspapers. We have become accustomed to shorter paragraphs.

## Students Quickly Become Skillful and Competent Editors

Your student editors are going to enjoy learning the proper professional editorial markings. The markings are simple, they are interesting, and they are fun to learn. By the time the editors use each one of the markings a few times in editing stories, they will be proficient in the use of them.

Printed on Page 62

# Professional Editorial Information Sheet

| | | |
|---|---|---|
| **CENTER** ][ | **Before:** | This line should be centered ] in relation to the lines above and below it. [ |
| | **After:** | This line should be centered in relation to the lines above and below it. |
| **CLOSE UP** ⌣ | **Before:** | The dog ran far away into the dis tance. |
| | **After:** | The dog ran far away into the distance. |
| **COMMA** ⌄ | **Before:** | If you want a comma here mark it on the paper. |
| | **After:** | If you want a comma here, mark it on the paper. |
| **DELETE** ℓ | **Before:** | The girl sang a beauttiful song. |
| | **After:** | The girl sang a beautiful song. |
| **HYPHEN** ⁼/ | **Before:** | She was a self reliant person. |
| | **After:** | She was a self-reliant person. |
| **INDENT** ⊐⊐ | **Before:** | The strong wind blew the boy's kite so high in the tree that he could not reach it. |
| | **After:** | The strong wind blew the boy's kite so high in the tree that he could not reach it. |
| **INSERTS** | | Insertions should be written on a separate piece of paper, then attached to the manuscript page and labeled "insert." Also mark a line to the place in the text where the insert should be placed. |
| **LET IT STAND** stet | **Before:** | Many red and ~~golden~~ apples fell from the trees. *yellow* stet |
| | **After:** | Many red and golden apples fell from the trees. |
| **LOWER CASE** lc | **Before:** | John caught sight of the ᏒᎯIᏒᏴᎾᏔ. lc |
| | **After:** | John caught sight of the rainbow. |
| **PARAGRAPH** ¶ | **Before:** | A paragraph is indicated by a special mark so every-one will know where the changes are made. ¶ |
| | **After:** | A paragraph is indicated by a special mark so everyone will know where the changes are made. |
| **PERIOD** ⊙ | **Before:** | The ring was set with diamonds and pearls ⊙ |
| | **After:** | The ring was set with diamonds and pearls. |
| **QUOTATION MARKS** ⌄⁶⁶ | **Before:** | He said, No!" ⁶⁶ |
| | **After:** | He said, "No!" |
| **SPACE** # | **Before:** | You can see whatis wrong here. # |
| | **After:** | You can see what is wrong here. |
| **TRANSPOSE** tr | **Before:** | The kind best of candy is fudge. tr |
| | **After:** | The best kind of candy is fudge. |
| **UPPERCASE** ≡ | **Before:** | This word should be in all capital letters. ≡ |
| | **After:** | This WORD should be in all capital letters. |

Because your students will know their classmates are going to see the marks they make, they will want those marks to be correct. As we have discovered, peer pressure can be a wonderful teaching tool.

## How Editors Should Read and Edit Other Students' Manuscripts

**Tell your students the following procedures for reading and editing other students' manuscripts:**

1. Be relaxed and rested when editing. Remember — The writer has worked diligently on the paper you are about to read. That writer deserves your undivided attention to his or her work, which is the same kind of respect you hope your editors will grant to your writing.

2. Now look carefully at the cover of the manuscript and read the title of the paper.

3. Turn the page and find out what audience the writer has designated. Then move yourself mentally into that audience, because you should try to read the paper from that audience's viewpoint and range of interest. Before making a mark on any line or word, first read the total manuscript from beginning to end.

4. Now place the PROFESSIONAL EDITORIAL INFORMATION SHEET where you can easily refer to it. Begin editing the manuscript thoughtfully, carefully, and precisely. Your function as an editor is to help the writer improve the paper.

5. After you have finished editing the manuscript, STOP. Clear your mind and read through it once more. Make sure your suggestions and markings are clear, readable, and constructive. Then write *positive* comments where you think they are deserved.

   **Remember — No negatives!**
   **Positive! Positive! Positive!**
   **Terrific! Fantastic!**
   **Beautifully written!**

6. Then sign your name as the editor of the manuscript.

## It's Time To Put Your Editors To Work

Now have each Continuing Editor begin reading and editing their respective student's manuscript. Allow them to work for the remainder of the hour and, if need be, continue through the next class period. These hours of editing become very active learning times for all students, not only in how to edit correctly, but in how to write better and more effectively. It also provides valuable time for the teacher to read and edit manuscripts and answer necessary questions.

*If you treat your students as professionals, they will act like professionals.*

*Give them good information and hands-on experiences, and they will learn. You won't need to give them tests.*

DO NOT allow editors to take their writers' manuscripts home, because some students will lose anything that isn't nailed to the walls or glued inside their back pockets. And in order to keep the papers from being blown from a school bus window or chewed up by someone's dog, each day have all students hand in their manuscripts at the end of the class period.

## The Advantages of Being a Continuing Editor

There are definite advantages in being a Continuing Editor who edits every manuscript that is written by one writer. The Continuing Editor has the opportunity to see the improvements in a particular writer's work, learn the writing style of that writer, and develop a personal interest in the student's progress.

## Pass the Edited Manuscripts to Other Students

After the Continuing Editors have edited the manuscripts, have them hand the papers to a second student. Now the second student reads the paper and considers the Continuing Editor's marks. The second student then adds anything he or she feels is needed.

Then each manuscript is passed to a third student, then a fourth. In two days of class time, every student should have the opportunity to read and edit four papers by other students and write encouraging comments and suggestions on those works.

## The Advantages of Your Students Editing More Than One Manuscript

**The advantages of editing several students' manuscripts are:**

1. The students get to see a variety of writing approaches and styles;

2. They have the opportunity to read works of varying quality;

3. They begin to realize that they are in a class with some very creative people, and they gain respect for some people whom they might otherwise not have noticed or even liked;

4. They see things in other writers' works that help them improve their own work;

5. Along with their own improvements, they see the other writers' skills are improving, too; and

6. They conclude they are lucky to be taking this course.

## The Advantages of Your Students Having More Than One Editor

**The advantages of having papers edited by more than one editor are:**

1. The writer's work receives more suggestions and corrections;

2. If the same suggestions are made by more than one editor, the writer will pay more attention to the comments; and

*Your students will begin to realize that they are in a class with some very creative people.*

3. It increases the possibility that all the students' manuscripts can receive suggestions and/or corrections that have been made by some of the more proficient editors in the class.

Note: You and I both know that some students have stronger backgrounds in literature, grammar, punctuation, spelling, and so forth. So having multiple editors, including the teacher, helps guarantee that each student's manuscripts will be read and edited by at least one editor who is more highly skilled.

As the course progresses, you will see your students' editorial skills improve, too. And some of the less skilled editors will move into the ranks of the more skilled ones.

On an ongoing basis, have your students make a list of the writers whose papers they read and edit. Before the course ends, you want every person to have the opportunity to read at least one paper by each of the other students.

During the editing periods, you also may want to take a few minutes to read aloud some fine sections that you have found in your students' writings. This is a wonderful opportunity to offer public attention and encouragement to those whom you feel deserve it and to those whom you feel need it. But only do this when your class is in the editing phase of their work. *Never* read anything aloud during the days when your students are writing creatively. Once they start writing an assignment, let them write with as few interruptions and as little spoken language as possible.

## When I Read and Edit Student Manuscripts

I never try to read and edit student manuscripts when I am tired, because I think my writers deserve my best consideration and advice. Therefore, I won't read their papers late at night. I will sit down and read them on Saturday or Sunday, or I will set the alarm clock for any day in the week at two or three o'clock in the morning, get up, and start reading. As I've said before, one of the main advantages of allowing students to edit during class is that it gives the teacher some time to edit, too. I always like that.

In selecting which papers I will read first, I do exactly as I did in the classroom. At my home, I line up all the papers on the fireplace mantle or on a couch or a table. Then I pick the one that has the most attractive and intriguing cover.

After reading the title and considering the audience, I read the manuscript from beginning to end, without making a mark on it. Then I go back to the beginning and edit the whole paper. By the time I've finished, my editorial markings may resemble a road map to the Panama Canal, but there never will be a negative word anywhere in the margins or between the lines.

ALL POSITIVES!

## No Exceptions for Teachers
## All Positives! — No Negatives!

After I read and edit my students' works, I find it is very easy to approach each writer and review that person's work with him or her, face to face. It is a joyous experience because I never write a negative comment on any-

*I never try to read and edit students' manuscripts when I am tired, because I think my writers deserve my very best consideration and advice.*

one's work. I believe my function as a teacher is to improve the work, not destroy the person. Negatives are destructive to the creative spirit. If my comments are positive and the editing has potential for improving the work, students realize this and are always open to suggestions. Even better, they appreciate my constructive criticism and suggestions.

It is my opinion that almost any idiot can tell others the things that may be wrong with a manuscript. But it takes a very astute and caring person to figure out ways to correct what is wrong and to make positive suggestions that will help a writer overcome his or her problems.

## The Brightest, Boldest Color You Can Find!

Teachers often ask me if I think they should stop using red ink when they mark editorial comments on student manuscripts.

"Use the brightest, boldest color you can find," I tell them. "If you are writing *only positive statements* on your students' works, I want these statements to stand out. No student is ever upset with the color of the ink when *Terrific! Splendid! Brilliant!* are written on the paper. But, I warn you — *negatives* stand out in *any* color in which they are written. And beginning writers do not deserve negatives that appear in any color or even in shades of gray."

## Your Students' Manuscripts Will Help You Develop Meaningful Lesson Plans

*The mistakes in your students' manuscripts will help you prepare very effective lesson plans that fit their needs.*

As you read and edit your students' manuscripts, you will find their papers to be exceedingly helpful to you in preparing effective lesson plans. Since student manuscripts will indicate clearly, the writers' most frequent mistakes and pressing needs, you can use this information to formulate and adjust your lesson plans to effective address their particular problems.

Make a list of these problems so you can discuss them in class and offer ways to solve them. By using the problems in their manuscripts as examples, the information you give to your students will now become more personal and important to them.

Because your students NEED and WANT these pieces of information to improve their writing, they will pay closer attention to what you are tyring to teach them.

Now they NEED and WANT to know where commas and periods go!

Now they NEED and WANT to use the right verb tenses!

Now they NEED and WANT to know the difference between a simple sentence and a complex one!

Now they NEED and WANT to know when it is better to use first-person, second-person, or third-person narrative!

And so on.

You have created an urgency within your students to learn. And it is a thousand times more exciting and fun to teach students who NEED and WANT to learn. For them, you have turned writing and editing, and the rules of grammar and punctuation into real life experiences.

Make the most of it!

## After the Manuscripts Have Been Edited

I always look forward to the day when all the manuscripts have been edited. Everyone is eagerly and nervously waiting to see what comments and corrections their Continuing Editors and the other student editors have written on their manuscripts.

**Each time, before the manuscripts are returned to the writers, ask the following questions:**

While you were editing the manuscripts, what was the *worst thing* that happened to you?

The answers will vary:

"I was afraid I wasn't doing a good enough job."

"You'll get better," you answer.

"I had to use the dictionary a lot to correct spelling and find the meanings of words."

"That's what dictionaries are for," you tell them.

"I liked the stories so much. But I wished I had known more about English."

"You will," you answer.

"I sometimes got so interested in the writing that I forgot to edit."

"I know what you mean," you smile.

And so on.

While you were editing the manuscripts, what was the *best thing* that happened to you?

"I found the stories were really interesting."

"So did I," you say.

"I am really glad I got to read John's paper. It's just great!"

"I think so, too," you agree.

"I really enjoyed making good suggestions."

"Me, too," you comment.

"In some of the papers, I found the very same mistakes I had been making in mine."

"That's good," you say, "because once you recognize those kinds of mistakes, you will start correcting them in your own writing, too."

**Now hand out the edited manuscripts to their respective writers.**

I always give the students time in class to read the editorial comments and markings, including mine, on all the copies of their papers. Then I allow time for the writers to meet with their Continuing Editors to discuss the editorial suggestions that were made. Of course, this means each person has two meetings, one as a writer and one as a Continuing Editor for another person. I don't have writers take the time to meet with their other student editors to discuss editorial markings, except in unusual situations.

I am always happy to answer questions the writers may have, either about my editorial markings or those made by any of their editors.

I love it when two or three students have made some of the same suggestions I have. That really gets me off the hook!

*I love it when two or three students have made some of the same suggestions I have. That really gets me off the hook!*

Sometimes it happens, but it is very rare, when a student writer complains because he or she feels an editor has edited too much. Most often, the opposite is the case. A student will complain because he or she feels that an editor has not edited *enough*. They really feel cheated if their editors have not been thorough.

Either situation gives you the opportunity to re-emphasize to your editors how very important their editorial markings and comments are to the writers. Again, make it clear that editors need to be diligent in giving their very best attention and skills to a writer's work.

Best of all, both the writers and the editors are reminded that they are responsible, not only to their teacher, but to each other. That realization alone changes the dynamics of this writing course.

## Improve and Complete the Manuscripts

Now instruct your writers to use their editors' suggestions and markings to assist themselves in correcting and improving their finished manuscripts. No, they do not have to use all the editorial suggestions, only those with which they agree.

*By now, your writers are better prepared to edit and improve their own manuscripts, for they have had the experience of editing four other writers' works.*

The writer has final decision as to what is included or excluded in his or her final manuscript. By now, your writers are better prepared to edit and improve their own manuscripts, for they have had the experience of editing four other writers' works. From this point on, you will see how learning to edit improves their writing skills.

Let your students use the remainder of the class period to work on organizing the improvements for and rewriting of their manuscripts. Tell them to complete their papers tonight because tomorrow, you will give them a new assignment.

Or you may choose to allow another day of class time for your students to work on improving their manuscripts. Always keep in mind, of course, that you want to give them enough time to do a good job, but not so much time that they drift and waiver from the work.

After your students correct and improve their manuscripts, whether or not you read them again, you at least will want to see the works and make note that the manuscripts have been completed. Then instruct your students to place their papers in their notebooks for safekeeping. Or if you really want to guarantee the safety of the works, set up a file in a cabinet or storage box and retain the manuscripts yourself. The choice is yours.

Your students are off to a good start.

THE BEST IS YET TO COME!

# Two Down and Ten To Go!

*You now have writers, editors, and a publishing company. You are on your way!*

You now have writers, you have editors, and you have a publishing company. With *two assignments* down and ten more to go, you are on your way.

## The Sequence of Assignments

I urge you to make the assignments in the order they are numbered and presented in this book. They are not placed in this sequence by a random hop, skip, and miss approach. The order in which they are presented is a result of careful thought and consideration.

Our goal is to expand and contract your students' thinking processes and to move them back and forth from an intense creative brain activity to an intense academic brain activity. An assignment which enlists a high degree of imagination is followed directly by an assignment that demands your writers to deal with factual information. In essence, you are presenting a process that both alternates and combines the functions of the students' academic brains and the functions of their creative brains.

**Printed on Page 70**

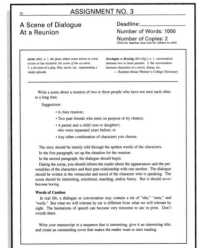

## ASSIGNMENT SHEET NO. 3 — A SCENE OF DIALOGUE AT A REUNION

Your students should really enjoy this assignment because a reunion scene offers so many possibilities. It is not just interesting; it is fascinating to put people together who have not seen each other for a number of years.

Your students should be able to easily write good dialogue, because they have heard so much dialogue in movies and on television shows. In all probability, they have heard more spoken dialogue than any other generation in the history of the world.

The problem, however, is that much of the movie and television dialogue they have heard has not been on the level of a Shakespeare or an Arthur Miller. I fear that the quality of most of it has fallen somewhere between afternoon soap operas and *Beavis and Butt-Head*.

# ASSIGNMENT NO. 3

## A Scene of Dialogue
## At a Reunion

Deadline:_____

**Number of Words: 1000**

**Number of Copies: 2**
(One for teacher and one for others to edit)

---

**scene** (sēn), *n.* 1. the place where some action or event occurs or has occurred: *the scene of the accident.* 5. a division of a play, film, novel, etc., representing a single episode.

**di·a·logue** or **di·a·log** (dī′ə-lôg′), *n.* 1. conversation between two or more persons. 2. the conversation between characters in a novel, drama, etc.
— Random House Webster's College Dictionary

---

Write a scene about a reunion of two or three people who have not seen each other in a long time.

Suggestions:

- A class reunion;

- Two past friends who meet on purpose or by chance;

- A parent and a child (son or daughter);
  who were separated years before; or

- Any other combination of characters you choose.

The story should be mainly told through the spoken words of the characters.

In the first paragraph, set up the situation for the reunion.

In the second paragraph, the dialogue should begin.

During the scene, you should inform the reader about the appearances and the personalities of the characters and their past relationship with one another. The dialogue should be written in the vernacular and mood of the character who is speaking. The scene should be interesting, emotional, touching, and/or funny. But it should *never* become boring.

**Words of Caution**

In real life, a dialogue or conversation may contain a lot of "uhs," "ums," and "wells." But what we will tolerate by ear is different from what we will tolerate by sight. The hesitations of speech can become very tiresome to see in print. Don't overdo them.

Write your manuscript in a sequence that is interesting, give it an interesting title, and create an outstanding cover that makes the reader want to start reading.

At any rate, your students have seen thousands of plots and a lot of scenes where people are talking, and they have heard real people talk at home, at school, and wherever else they have been. Your students have had years of verbal input, so they should be well-prepared and primed to create some very interesting scenes with dialogue.

Once your students know they are going to write dialogue, their "antennae" will go up. They will start listening more intently to what people say to each other and how characters talk on television and in movies.

## He Said, She Said

Before I hand out copies of ASSIGNMENT SHEET NO. 3 — A SCENE OF DIALOGUE AT A REUNION, I always stress to my students the immense variety of words, including those used as synonyms, that are available in the English language. I think it is a good idea for you to do the same.

**Begin by telling your students:**

A synonym is a word that means the same or nearly the same as another word.

**Then write on the chalkboard, the word: SAID**

Then give your students about ten minutes to make individual lists of at least twenty synonyms that mean the same as *Said*, such as *spoke*, *stated*, *replied*, *asked*, and *answered*. Have one student read his or her list of twenty aloud as you write the words on the board. Then ask other students what words they have on their lists, and write down any additional synonyms they offer. After about fifty different words, stop.

Are there more than fifty synonyms for *Said?* Yes, there are many more, but fifty will make the point.

Make it clear to your students that you expect them to use a variety of the synonyms for *"said"* in their scenes of dialogue, but not to overdo it to the point that the reading is slowed or becomes awkward.

## Quotation Marks Are the
## Same As Cartoon Balloons

Some students have difficulty in trying to figure out where to place quotation marks. So I ask them if they read comic strips. They tell me yes.

Then I ask them if they ever have noticed the balloons that are in the comic strips. Most know what I'm talking about, but to make sure, I quickly draw a comic face on the board and say, "This is Mike." Then I draw a balloon coming out of Mike's mouth and write something inside the balloon, such as, "Wow! What a great day!"

The students can see that the balloon encloses what Mike is saying.

"Balloons are the quotation marks in comic strips," I tell them.

Now I write Mike's comment on the board. But I don't draw a balloon around it. Instead, I enclose his comment within quotation marks and write who said it:

**❝**Wow! What a great day!**❞** exclaimed Mike.

*Your students have had years of verbal input, so they should be well-prepared and primed to create some very interesting scenes with dialogue.*

Simple and easy? You bet it is! Your students will immediately understand what you have said, and they will remember it.

**Now give each student a copy of:**
**ASSIGNMENT SHEET NO. 3 — A SCENE OF DIALOGUE (Reunion).**
**Read the Assignment Sheet aloud and explain the information.**

**Be sure to give your students the date of the deadline, and tell them:**
*CONQUER THE POWER OF THE WHITE!*
Start writing!

You know the procedure. Let them start writing. After a few minutes, walk around the room and give them instant approval.

They write their manuscripts. The manuscripts are edited, with corrections and constructive suggestions given.

After the manuscripts are corrected and refined, either you store the manuscripts or have your students keep them in their notebooks.

Then you are ready to present the next assignment to your students.

## ASSIGNMENT SHEET NO. 4 — AN EDITORIAL

I would start this session by reading a couple of editorials to the class or provide copies of those editorials for your students to read silently. And/or assign your students to read several newspaper or magazine editorials and bring them to class. *USA Today* is an excellent source as are your local newspapers and national news magazines, such as *Time* and *Newsweek*.

Urge your students to write their editorials on subjects about which they feel passionate. If they do, you can expect to see a larger quantity of high-voltage adjectives, power-packed vocabularies, and super-charged statements of facts and opinions.

As writers, this is a marvelous personal thinking assignment for your students, because they will be telling about their interests, their viewpoints, and how they think and form their opinions. Then, as editors, they will be able to discover how strongly their classmates feel about certain subjects. This always brings about some interesting interactions between the students. It also offers another excellent opportunity for you to become even better acquainted with how and what your students think.

**Now give each student a copy of:**
**ASSIGNMENT SHEET NO. 4 — AN EDITORIAL.**
**Read the Assignment Sheet aloud and explain the information.**

**Be sure to give your students the date of the deadline, and tell them:**
*CONQUER THE POWER OF THE WHITE!*
Start writing!

You know the procedure. Let them start writing. After a few minutes, walk around the room and give them instant approval.

They write their manuscripts. The manuscripts are edited, with corrections and constructive suggestions given.

After the manuscripts are corrected and refined, either you store the manuscripts or have your students keep them in their notebooks.

Then you are ready to present the next assignment to your students.

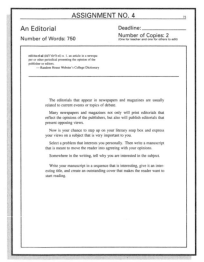

Printed on Page 73

*You can expect a larger quantity of high-voltage adjectives and power-packed vocabularies in your students' editorials.*

## An Editorial

**Number of Words: 750**

Deadline:_____

**Number of Copies: 2**
(One for teacher and one for others to edit)

---

**ed·i·to·ri·al** (ĕd′ĭ′tôr′ē-əl) *n.* 1. an article in a newspaper or other periodical presenting the opinion of the publisher or editors.

---

The editorials that appear in newspapers and magazines are usually related to current events or topics of debate.

Many newspapers and magazines not only will print editorials that reflect the opinions of the publishers, but also will publish editorials that present opposing views.

Now is your chance to step up on your literary soap box and express your views on a subject that is very important to you.

Select a problem that interests you personally. Then write a manuscript that is meant to move the reader into agreeing with your opinions.

Somewhere in the writing, tell why you are interested in the subject.

Write your manuscript in a sequence that is interesting, give it an interesting title, and create an outstanding cover that makes the reader want to start reading.

# Down to Basics!
## The Beginning, Middle, and End

The best advice anyone can give a beginning writer is:
**Tell it simply.  Tell it well.**

## ASSIGNMENT SHEET NO. 5 — A CHILDREN'S STORY

*This assignment is so much fun because it urges writers to write the kinds of stories they enjoyed as children.*

This assignment is one of my personal favorites, because it is so much fun to write!  It's fun because it urges writers to review their own childhoods and inspires them to write the kinds of stories they enjoyed as children.

Quite simply, the objective of this assignment is to write a piece of entertainment for children.  The more entertaining the story, the more fun it will be for children to read.

The opportunity to write for children is very beneficial to students.  Much stress is removed, because the writers are not asked to develop profound statements nor use elaborate or extended vocabularies.  Instead, they are given the freedom to tell their stories in simpler language, encouraged to use their imaginations, and allowed to utilize their skills as storytellers.

## The Ten-Minute College Course

Before you give *A Children's Story* assignment sheet to your students, you need to teach them a *college course* in *The Three Basic Elements of a Good Story*.

I know it's a college course because I took it.  The only difference in the course I sat through and the one you will teach is the amount of time you will take in presenting it.  The course I took lasted fourteen weeks.  But you can teach all the important parts of that course in less than *ten minutes*!  All you are going to do is cut out hours of tedium and hours of needless chitchat about Hemingway, Faulkner, Fitzgerald, the Brontës, and all those other great writers, and get down to the basics.

The basic elements of a good story are so simple that you can teach them to second graders.  But it's more fun to teach them to sixth graders; even more fun to teach them to eighth graders; and far more fun to teach them to high school and college students.  I even have a wonderful time teaching them to teachers.  You'll see what I mean.

## The Three Basic Elements of a Good Story

Now, tell your students you are going to teach them:
### THE THREE BASIC ELEMENTS OF A GOOD STORY

Ask your students if they know the first basic element.  **If they do not know the answer, after a short pause, you tell them:**

The word we are looking for is — **BEGINNING.**

Every good story needs a good **BEGINNING.**

Once everyone knows the first basic element, the other two elements are obvious — a **MIDDLE** and an **END.**

**Write all three on the chalkboard:**
> **BEGINNING**
> **MIDDLE**
> **END**

What should a good **BEGINNING** present?

A good **BEGINNING** presents the **SETTING** and the **CHARACTERS.**

If the story is to be interesting, what does the **MIDDLE** need?

An interesting **MIDDLE** should have a **PROBLEM** or a **CONFLICT.**

What needs to happen before the **END**?

The **PROBLEM** should be **SOLVED.**

Or the **CONFLICT** must be **RESOLVED.**

**Simple! Simple! Simple!**

*Every good story contains three basic elements. They are easy to teach and easy to remember.*

## Two Other Ingredients

There are TWO OTHER INGREDIENTS for every good story.  Whether the story is a tragedy or a comedy, it should contain —

some **SERIOUSNESS** and some **HUMOR.**

All classic comedies have their SERIOUS moments.  George S. Kaufman, Charlie Chaplin, and Neil Simon demonstrated they understood that.

And most serious stories are enhanced if they contain moments of HUMOR.  Shakespeare definitely knew this.  Although both *Hamlet* and *MacBeth* are tragedies, they contain some very funny lines and humorous situations within their plots.

## Examples of the Basic Elements of a Good Story

*The Three Little Pigs* is a perfect story to use as an example of the basic elements of a good story, because everyone knows the story and the elements are so obvious.

**You may read the following aloud or tell students in your own words:**

In the BEGINNING of *The Three Little Pigs*, the central CHARACTERS are quickly introduced while they are leaving home to seek their fortunes.

The SETTING is in the country. How do we know that? We know because most pigs live in the country, and the three little pigs weren't told to get building permits before they built their houses.

In the MIDDLE, the PROBLEM arises with the introduction of the villain, a big bad wolf. He is undoubtedly the PROBLEM, and the CONFLICT is very clear — there is a killer on the loose, and he is after the three little pigs!

*Once the three little pigs get rid of the big bad wolf, the PROBLEM is solved and the CONFLICT is resolved.*

*Therefore, the story is immediately concluded — it's the END.*

Once the three little pigs get rid of the big bad wolf, the PROBLEM is solved and the CONFLICT is resolved. Therefore, the story is immediately concluded — it's the END.

Within the story, there is both SERIOUSNESS and HUMOR.

SERIOUSNESS — For the characters, it's a matter of life or death. Who's going to have lunch? Or who's going to live another day?

HUMOR — There is a very funny line that is used three times — *"Not by the hair of my chinny-chin-chin!"* It is very difficult for anyone to read that line without smiling. I think even *"I'll huff and I'll puff, and I'll blow your house down!"* injects humor, too, because *huff* and *puff* are fun words and they rhyme.

## Another Example

**You can use any story to demonstrate the basic elements of a good story, even a nursery rhyme:**

BEGINNING — *"Little Miss Muffet sat on her tuffet."*

The CHARACTER, Miss Muffet, is introduced, and she is sitting on the SETTING, a tuffet, *"eating her curds and whey."* She is eating breakfast.

MIDDLE — Here comes the PROBLEM and the CONFLICT — *"Along came a spider and sat down beside her."*

The PROBLEM is — The spider might bite her. As we know, getting bitten hurts and some spiders are poisonous.

That causes the CONFLICT between Miss Muffet and the spider. Miss Muffet is frightened.

*Miss Muffet solves the PROBLEM and resolves the CONFLICT.*

Miss Muffet solves the PROBLEM and resolves the CONFLICT by jumping up and running away.

Where is the SERIOUSNESS in the story? The more poisonous the spider, the more serious the PROBLEM. The more venomous the bite, the more compelling the CONFLICT.

What's HUMOROUS in the story? Readers tend to think it is funny when a person is frightened by something, especially if that something is smaller than the person. Although it is not in the story, I think most readers imagine that when Miss Muffet sees the spider, she lets out a bloodcurdling scream, throws her curds and whey into the air, and runs like spit! And that makes it even funnier!

In ten minutes, you have taught a full college course in:

### THE THREE BASIC ELEMENTS OF A GOOD STORY

These three basic elements are so simple, your students will remember them always. So don't give them a test. That only would insult their intelligence and make them wonder about yours.

## ASSIGNMENT SHEET NO. 5 — A CHILDREN'S STORY

**Now give each student a copy of:**
**ASSIGNMENT SHEET NO. 5 — A CHILDREN'S STORY.**
**Read the Assignment Sheet aloud and explain the information.**

Be sure to give your students the date of the deadline, and have them write it on their copies.

**After you have finished reading, tell them:**

### CONQUER THE POWER OF THE WHITE!

Start writing!

You know the procedure. Let them start writing. After a few minutes, walk around the room and give them instant approval.

They write their manuscripts. The manuscripts are edited, with corrections and constructive suggestions given.

After the manuscripts are corrected and refined, you will want to see the works. Then either you store the manuscripts or have your students retain a copy of their manuscripts in their notebooks.

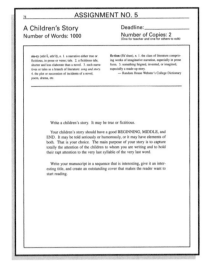

Printed on Page 78

## An Extra Plus for Your Writers of Children's Stories!

Once your students' stories for children are written, edited, and refined, you might wish to assign every writer to read his or her story to a child or to a group of children.

If you want the readings to become exciting events, then you should arrange for all your writers to go to an elementary school and read their stories aloud in the classrooms.

Then have your writers answer any questions the children might ask. The children are sure to ask a lot of questions about the author and how he or she wrote the story.

By the time the sessions are over, your authors will have experienced an hour of fame and will be *"walking on air!"*

*AUTHOR! AUTHOR! After the children's stories are completed, you can have your authors read their manuscripts to groups of children.*

## A Children's Story
### Number of Words: 1000

Deadline:_____

### Number of Copies: 2
(One for teacher and one for others to edit)

---

**sto·ry** (stôr′ē, stōr′ē), *n.* 1. a narrative either true or fictitious, in prose or verse; tale. 2. a fictitious tale, shorter and less elaborate than a novel. 3. such narratives or tales as a branch of literature: *song and story.* 4. the plot or succession of incidents of a novel, poem, drama, etc.

**fic·tion** (fĭk′shən), *n.* 1. the class of literature comprising works of imaginative narration, especially in prose form. 3. something feigned, invented, or imagined, especially a made-up story.
— Random House Webster's College Dictionary

---

Write a children's story. It may be true or fictitious.

Your children's story should have a good BEGINNING, MIDDLE, and END. It may be told seriously or humorously, or it may have elements of both. That is your choice. The main purpose of your story is to capture totally the attention of the children to whom you are writing and to hold their rapt attention to the very last syllable of the very last word.

Write your manuscript in a sequence that is interesting, give it an interesting title, and create an outstanding cover that makes the reader want to start reading.

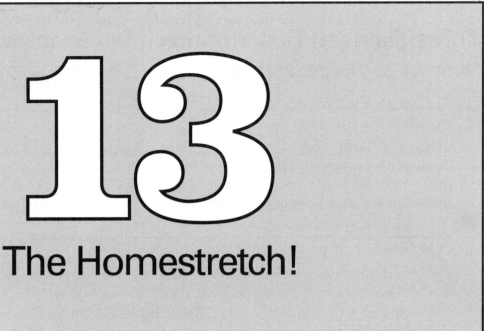

# The Homestretch!

By now your students should be writing and editing like gangbusters!

Their writing skills are improving. Their thinking skills are improving. They know how to edit. They know how to correct and refine manuscripts.

From here on in, you and your students are in the homestretch.

## ASSIGNMENT SHEET NO. 6 — THREE DETAILED DESCRIPTIONS

This assignment draws your writers' attention to details and has them write about three of them.

The first two details will be descriptions that are written from the viewpoint of a detective. The third detailed description poses a challenge, because the writers must not tell the name of the thing they are describing.

**Now give each student a copy of:**

**ASSIGNMENT SHEET NO. 6 — THREE DETAILED DESCRIPTIONS.**

**Read the Assignment Sheet aloud and explain the information.**

Be sure you give your students the date of the deadline, and have them write it on their copies.

**After you have finished reading, tell them:**

*CONQUER THE POWER OF THE WHITE!*

Start writing!

You know the procedure. Let them start writing. After a few minutes, walk around the room and give them instant approval.

They write their manuscripts. The manuscripts are edited, with corrections and constructive suggestions given.

After the manuscripts are corrected and refined, you will want to see the works. Then either you store the manuscripts or have your students retain a copy of their manuscripts in their notebooks.

Now you are ready to present the next assignment to your students.

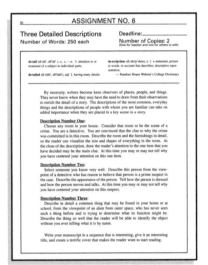

Printed on Page 80

*"Keen observations are elementary, my dear Watson."*
*— S. Holmes*

## Three Detailed Descriptions
Number of Words: 250 each

Deadline:_____

Number of Copies: 2
(One for teacher and one for others to edit)

---

**de·tail** (dĭ-tāl′, dē′tāl′ ), *n., v.,* —*n.* 3. attention to or treatment of a subject in individual parts.

**de·tailed** (dĭ-tāld′, dē′tāld′), *adj.* 2. having many details.

**de·scrip·tion** (dĭ-skrĭp′shən), *n.* 1. a statement, picture in words, or account that describes; descriptive representation.
— Random House Webster's College Dictionary

---

By necessity, writers become keen observers of places, people, and things. They never know when they may have the need to draw from their observations to enrich the detail of a story. The descriptions of the most common, everyday things and the descriptions of people with whom you are familiar can take on added importance when they are placed in a key scene in a story.

### Description Number One:

Choose any room in your house. Consider that room to be the scene of a crime. You are a detective. You are convinced that the clue to why the crime was committed is in this room. Describe the room and the furnishings in detail, so the reader can visualize the size and shapes of everything in the room. At the close of the description, draw the reader's attention to the one item that you have decided may be the main clue. At this time you may or may not tell why you have centered your attention on this one item.

### Description Number Two:

Select someone you know very well. Describe this person from the viewpoint of a detective who has reason to believe that person is a prime suspect in the case. Describe the appearance of the person. Tell how the person is dressed and how the person moves and talks. At this time you may or may not tell why you have centered your attention on this suspect.

### Description Number Three:

Describe in detail a common thing that may be found in your home or at school, from the viewpoint of an alien from outer space, who has never seen such a thing before and is trying to determine what its function might be. Describe the thing so well that the reader will be able to identify the object without you ever telling what it is by name.

Write your manuscript in a sequence that is interesting, give it an interesting title, and create a terrific cover that makes the reader want to start reading.

## ASSIGNMENT SHEET NO. 7 — AN ESSAY

An essay can be a lot of fun to write. The students pick a topic and write as many things as they can think of and everything they can find out about the subject.

**Now give each student a copy of:**
**ASSIGNMENT SHEET NO. 7 — AN ESSAY.**
**Read the Assignment Sheet aloud and explain the information.**

Be sure to give your students the date of the deadline, and have them write it on their copies.

**After you have finished reading, tell them:**
*CONQUER THE POWER OF THE WHITE!*
Start writing!

You know the procedure. Let them start writing. After a few minutes, walk around the room and give them instant approval.

They write their manuscripts. The manuscripts are edited, with corrections and constructive suggestions given.

After the manuscripts are corrected and refined, you will want to see the works. Then either you store the manuscripts or have your students retain a copy of their manuscripts in their notebooks.

Now you are ready to present the next assignment to your students.

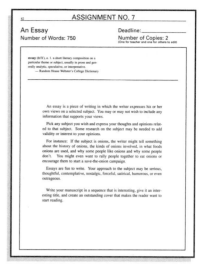
Printed on Page 82

## ASSIGNMENT SHEET NO. 8 — A NEWS ARTICLE ABOUT THE REUNION SCENE

Another terrific exercise in creative thinking! In this assignment, students retell the same story they told in their *Scene of Dialogue At a Reunion*, but this time from a different viewpoint — a news story. You might want to suggest that they read two or three news stories before they begin writing.

**Now give each student a copy of:**
**ASSIGNMENT SHEET NO. 8 — A NEWS ARTICLE (Reunion).**
**Read the Assignment Sheet aloud and explain the information.**

Be sure you give your students the date of the deadline, and have them write it on their copies.

Note: Information about the *Five W's* and the *H* is on the Assignment Sheet, and there also is an example of a news story.

**After you have finished reading, tell your students:**
*CONQUER THE POWER OF THE WHITE!*
Start writing!

You know the procedure. Let them start writing. After a few minutes, walk around the room and give them instant approval.

They write their manuscripts. The manuscripts are edited, with corrections and constructive suggestions given.

After the manuscripts are corrected and refined, you will want to see the works. Then either you store the manuscripts or have your students retain a copy of their manuscripts in their notebooks.

Now you are ready to present the next assignment to your students.

Printed on Page 83

*Another terrific exercise in creative thinking!*

## An Essay
## Number of Words: 750

Deadline:_____

## Number of Copies: 2
(One for teacher and one for others to edit)

es·say (ĕs′ā′), *n*. 1. a short literary composition on a
particular theme or subject, usually in prose and gen-
erally analytic, speculative, or interpretative.
    — Random House Webster's College Dictionary

An essay is a piece of writing in which the writer expresses his or her own views on a selected subject. You may or may not wish to include any information that supports your views.

Pick any subject you wish and express your thoughts and opinions related to that subject. Some research on the subject may be needed to add validity or interest to your opinions.

For instance: If the subject is onions, the writer might tell something about the history of onions, the kinds of onions involved, in what foods onions are used, and why some people like onions and why some people don't. You might even want to rally people together to eat onions or encourage them to start a save-the-onion campaign.

Essays are fun to write. Your approach to the subject may be serious, thoughtful, contemplative, nostalgic, forceful, satirical, humorous, or even outrageous.

Write your manuscript in a sequence that is interesting, give it an interesting title, and create an outstanding cover that makes the reader want to start reading.

# ASSIGNMENT NO. 8

## A News Article About The Reunion Scene

Deadline:_____
Number of Words: 225
Number of Copies: 2
(One for teacher and one for others to edit)

---

**news** (nōoz, nyōoz), *n.* 2. a report on recent or new events in a newspaper or other periodical, or on radio or television

**ar·ti·cle** (är′tĭ-kel), *n.* 1. a factual piece of writing, usually on a single topic, appearing in a newspaper, magazine, etc.

---

Write a news article about your reunion dialogue scene as if it were a real or factual event. The format of the article is simple and precise.

In the first paragraph of the article, the writer should interject all of the Five W's of Who, What, When, Where, and Why, along with the One H of How, if How is needed to tell the most important facts. Each succeeding paragraph adds details that are less important information than the one that precedes it.

Using the information of eye witnesses, the reporter's job is to tell the story matter-of-factly without interjecting his or her own opinions or feelings.

When reading the following article, one can easily suppose what the scene might have been.

## Woman "Punches" Friend at Class Reunion

Last night the Tenth Reunion of the 1970 Senior Class was held in the Central High School gymnasium, where one of the attendees, Joyce Michaels, poured a bowl of punch over another attendee, Marilyn Bingert.

"I did it and I'm glad," said Ms. Michaels, an accountant who now resides in the upstate City of Poughkeepsie. "I wish I had done that ten years ago!"

"It happened so suddenly," said Paul Martin, who was standing nearby. "One minute they were just talking, and the next thing I knew, Joyce lifted the bowl and covered Marilyn with lime punch."

"Joyce is still jealous because Bill married me," said Ms. Bingert, a local beautician, as she wiped the punch from her sequined dress.

"It was a vicious attack," said Bill Bingert, Marilyn's husband. "I'm certainly glad I never married that woman," he said, referring to Ms. Michaels.

"It is difficult for me to believe that Joyce did such a thing," said Harriet Boseman, the high school's English teacher. "She was always such a shy, well-mannered girl."

Ms. Michaels left town early this morning. Ms. Bingert says she has not yet decided if she will file charges for assault.

Write your article, give it an interesting headline, and create an outstanding cover that makes the reader want to start reading.

# ASSIGNMENT NO. 9

## A Villain's Rebuttal
Number of Words: 750

Deadline:_____

Number of Copies: 2
(One for teacher and one for others to edit)

---

**vil·lain** (vĭl′ən), *n.* 1. a cruelly malicious person who is involved in or devoted to wickedness or crime; scoundrel. 2. a character in a play, novel, or the like, who constitutes an important evil agency in the plot.

**re·but** (rĭ-bŭt′), *n.* 1. to rebut by evidence or argument. 2. to oppose by contrary proof.

**re·but·tal** (rĭ-bŭt′l) *n.* 1. an act of rebutting, as in a debate.
— Random House Webster's College Dictionary

---

You are going to love this assignment!

In THE TRUE STORY OF THE THREE LITTLE PIGS BY A. WOLF, written by John Scieszka and illustrated by Alane Smith, the wolf tells the story of *The Three Little Pigs* from his viewpoint. You can be sure that the wolf remembers, or at least tells the story very differently from the one we have heard and read. In his rebuttal, the wolf tells how those mean little pigs caused all the trouble and blamed everything on him, poor thing.

Select a *very well-known* story, movie, or play and retell it from the viewpoint of the villain. And here is the fun part: Villains do not have to hold the truth as being sacred or place much value in their word of honor. So as you write from the villain's viewpoint, you may lie all you want.

Write your manuscript in a sequence that is interesting, give it an interesting title, and create an outstanding cover that makes the reader want to start reading.

# ASSIGNMENT NO. 9 —
# A VILLAIN'S REBUTTAL

For your students, this assignment will be the "pick of the litter" and the "hit" of the course. They probably will absolutely love it, because they get to retell a famous children's story or fairy tale from the viewpoint of the infamous villain. Everyone will want to read everyone else's paper.

Just make sure each writer chooses a story everyone else knows. I personally don't care if two or more writers select the same story and the same villain, because the finished manuscripts are bound to be very different from each other. However, if you prefer to have all the papers based on different stories, you should have your writers make their selections during class. You place the titles of the stories on the chalkboard, then do not allow anyone to use the same story.

**Now give each student a copy of:**
**ASSIGNMENT SHEET NO. 9 — A VILLAIN'S REBUTTAL.**
**Read the Assignment Sheet aloud and explain the information.**

Be sure you give your students the date of the deadline, and have them write it on their copies.

**After you have finished reading, tell them:**
*CONQUER THE POWER OF THE WHITE!*
Start writing!

You know the procedure. Let them start writing. After a few minutes, walk around the room and give them instant approval.

They write their manuscripts. The manuscripts are edited, with corrections and constructive suggestions given.

After the manuscripts are corrected and refined, you will want to see the works. Then either you store the manuscripts or have your students retain a copy of their manuscripts in their notebooks.

Now you are ready to present the next assignment to your students.

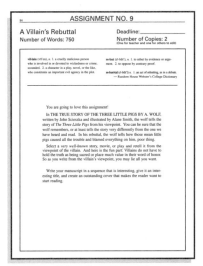

Printed on Page 84

*This assignment is bound to be the "pick of the litter."*

## The All-Time Great Villains Suggestion List

| Villain | Source | Villain | Source |
|---|---|---|---|
| Wolf | The Three Little Pigs | Wicked Queen | Snow White & the Seven Dwarfs |
| Stepmother | Cinderella | Giant | Jack and the Beanstalk |
| Cruella De Vil | 101 Dalmations | Fox | The Gingerbread Man |
| Wolf | Red Riding Hood | Sheriff of Nottingham | The Adventures of Robin Hood |
| Witch | Hansel and Gretel | Ebenezer Scrooge | A Christmas Carol |
| Dwarf | Rumpelstiltskin | Brombones | The Legend of Sleepy Hollow |
| Witch | Rapunzel | Spider | Little Miss Muffet |
| Long John Silver | Treasure Island | Darth Vader | Star Wars Trilogy |
| Brutus | Popeye | The Evil Fairy | The Sleeping Beauty |
| Count Dracula | Dracula | Injun Joe | The Adventures of Tom Sawyer |
| Shere Khan | The Jungle Book | Trolls | The Three Billy Goats Gruff |
| The Joker | Batman | Witch of the West | The Wizard of Oz |
| Bill Sikes | Oliver Twist | Captain Hook | The Story of Peter Pan |
| Dragon | The Hobbit | Mr. Hyde | Dr. Jekyll and Mr. Hyde |

Printed on Page 87

*Varying the viewpoints enhances creative thinking.*

Printed on Page 88

## ASSIGNMENT NO. 10 — THREE RESEARCH BRIEFS

This assignment is not going to be your students' favorite one, but they need the experience. Each student writer needs to select one *person*, one *place*, and one *event* about which he or she will write.

For your convenience, I have composed three lists. Each list is numbered 1 through 50, for the following topics:

1. NOTED PEOPLE
2. FAMOUS PLACES
3. HISTORICAL EVENTS

I find it is more venturesome for students when they have the experience of researching and writing about topics that are unfamiliar to them. So I suggest that you have them make their topic selections through random choices. For example:

For the selection of a *NOTED PERSON*, instruct your writers, one at a time, to say a number from 1 through 50. Then you read the name that is typed by that number on the list.

For the selection of a *FAMOUS PLACE,* have them say a number from 1 through 50, then tell them the corresponding place on the list.

Do likewise with numbers 1 through 50 when selecting *HISTORICAL EVENTS*.

All this can be done in minutes.

As you will see on the Assignment Sheet, what would otherwise be just encyclopedia-type biographies, descriptions, and/or definitions, the research briefs will instead be dynamically enhanced by the varying viewpoints of the writers.

**Now give each student a copy of:**
**ASSIGNMENT SHEET NO. 10 — THREE RESEARCH BRIEFS.**
**Read the Assignment Sheet aloud and explain the information.**

Be sure to give your students the date of the deadline, and have them write it on their copies.

> Note: There is an exception to this assignment. Once students have selected their three subjects, they may need to go to the library, because this time, they will need to do some research before they commence writing. In fact, you might want to take them to the library the day after you make the assignment.

**Once your students have finished researching their subjects, tell them:**
*CONQUER THE POWER OF THE WHITE!*
Start writing!

You know the procedure. Let them start writing. After a few minutes, walk around the room and give them instant approval.

They write their manuscripts. The manuscripts are edited, with corrections and constructive suggestions given.

After the manuscripts are corrected and refined, you will want to see the works. Then either you store the manuscripts or have your students retain a copy of their manuscripts in their notebooks.

Now you are ready to present the next assignment to your students.

## NOTED PEOPLE

1. P.T. Barnum
2. Robert E. Lee
3. Thomas Jefferson
4. Benjamin Franklin
5. Sequoya
6. Charles Lindbergh
7. Paul Revere
8. Elvis Presley
9. Hans Christian Andersen
10. Sir Winston Churchill
11. Abraham Lincoln
12. Eleanor Roosevelt
13. Henry Ford
14. Walter Cronkite
15. Jesse Owens
16. Franklin Delano Roosevelt
17. Jackie Robinson
18. Wolfgang Amadeus Mozart
19. Mahatma Gandhi
20. Thomas A. Edison
21. Dame Agatha Christie
22. Albert Schweitzer
23. Napoleon Bonaparte
24. Bob Hope
25. Dr. Martin Luther King
26. Babe Ruth
27. Jack the Ripper
28. Booker T. Washington
29. Michelangelo
30. Golda Meir
31. Frank Lloyd Wright
32. Florence Nightingale
33. Leonardo da Vinci
34. Albert Einstein
35. Jonas Salk
36. Mother Teresa
37. Cecil B. De Mille
38. Amelia Earhart
39. Gen. Douglas MacArthur
40. Blackbeard the Pirate
41. Norman Rockwell
42. John F. Kennedy
43. Robin Hood
44. Colonel Harland Sanders
45. Vincent van Gogh
46. Fred Astaire
47. Billy the Kid
48. Mario Andretti
49. William Shakespeare
50. Mark Twain

## FAMOUS PLACES

1. Cyberspace
2. Appomattox Courthouse
3. Monticello
4. Pan American Highway
5. Auschwitz Death Camp
6. Carlsbad Caverns
7. The Berlin Wall
8. Erie Canal
9. Mount Vernon
10. The Alamo
11. Epcot Center
12. Shangri-la
13. Disneyland
14. Great Wall of China
15. Camelot
16. Golden Gate Bridge
17. Jamestown Settlement, VA
18. Panama Canal
19. Loch Ness, Scotland
20. Ellis Island
21. Tower of London
22. Pompeii
23. Empire State Building
24. Berchtesgaden
25. Eiffel Tower
26. The Kremlin
27. The Sistine Chapel
28. Arlington National Cemetery
29. The Santa Fe Trail
30. Rocky Mountains
31. The Vietnam Memorial
32. Atlantis
33. Leaning Tower of Pisa
34. Hearst Castle, San Simeon
35. The Grand Canyon
36. Pyramids/Sphinx at Giza
37. Stonehenge
38. Ford's Theater
39. West Point Academy
40. The Mississippi River
41. Williamsburg, VA
42. Mount Rushmore
43. The Nile River
44. World Trade Center
45. Boulder Dam
46. Valley Forge
47. Niagara Falls
48. The Moon
49. Taj Mahal
50. The Statue of Liberty

## HISTORICAL EVENTS

1. First Man on the Moon
2. Sinking of the Titanic
3. Hindenburg Air Disaster
4. Signing of the Magna Carta
5. Oklahoma City Bombing
6. Nuremberg Trials, Germany
7. The Gold Rush
8. Battle of the Bulge
9. Exxon Valdez Oil Spill
10. Hiroshima/Nagasaki Bombing
11. Mardi Gras
12. Academy Awards (Oscar)
13. Olympic Games
14. Building of the Panama Canal
15. The Boston Tea Party
16. Hubble Space Telescope Launch
17. Paul Revere's Ride
18. Challenger Shuttle Disaster
19. Great Chicago Fire-1871
20. Pony Express Ride
21. War of the Worlds Broadcast
22. Oklahoma Land Run-1893
23. Bell's Telephone Invention
24. Breaking the Sound Barrier
25. Pocahontas Saves John Smith
26. Bombing of Pearl Harbor
27. World Series in Baseball
28. Betsy Ross Makes American Flag
29. Scopes Monkey Trial
30. Electric Light Bulb Invented
31. Battle of Gettysburg
32. Lewis and Clark Expedition
33. Wounded Knee Massacre
34. Transcontinental Railroad-1869
35. Landing of the Pilgrims
36. Indianapolis 500
37. Little Big Horn Battle
38. Signing-Declaration Independence
39. Extinction of the Dinosaurs
40. Bubonic Plague, London-1665
41. San Francisco Earthquake-1906
42. The Holocaust
43. Berlin Air Lift
44. Cuban Missile Crisis
45. Wright Brothers' First Flight
46. Battle of the Alamo
47. Columbus Discovers America
48. Ben Franklin's Kite Experiment
49. The Rose Bowl Parade
50. Building of Brooklyn Bridge

# ASSIGNMENT NO. 10

## Three Research Briefs
Number of Words: 250 each

Deadline:_____

Number of Copies: 2
(One for teacher and one for others to edit)

---

**re·search** (rĭ-sûrch′, rē′sûrch′), *n., v.,* —*n.* 1. diligent and systematic inquiry into a subject in order to discover or revise facts, theories, etc.

**brief** (brēf), *adj.* 2. using few words; concise: *a brief report.*
— Random House Webster's College Dictionary

---

Whether or not a writer is writing factual prose, he or she often has to research real facts about people, places, and events and then summarize the findings, without making readers feel as if they are reading a paragraph from an encyclopedia.

Your subjects are:

1. NOTED PEOPLE

2. FAMOUS PLACES

3. HISTORICAL EVENTS

Read about each of the three subjects, and then:

1. Write a brief biography of the noted person as if you know him or her well and are recommending that person to a friend as a potential dinner quest.

2. Write about the famous place as if you are a travel agent who is trying to persuade the reader to personally visit that famous place.

3. Write about the historical event as if you were there and witnessed it when it occurred.

The trick is to make the person, place, and event absolutely fascinating to the reader. You may use as many superlatives as you like.

Write your manuscript in a sequence that is interesting, give it an interesting title, and create an outstanding cover that makes the reader want to start reading.

# A Personal Remembrance
## Number of Words: 750

Deadline: _____

## Number of Copies: 2
(One for teacher and one for others to edit)

---

**per·son·al** (pûr′sə-nəl), *adj.* 1. of, pertaining to, or concerning a particular person; individual; private: *a personal opinion.*

**re·mem·brance** (rĭ-měm′brəns), *n.* 1. a retained mental impression; memory.
— Random House Webster's College Dictionary

---

All of us have moments or incidents in our pasts that we will never forget. Some of these moments are pleasant to remember; others are painful Some are sad, while others are wildly funny. Some memories we want to remember; others we wish we could forever blot from our minds.

Select an incident in your life that is special to you and one you would like to place into writing and share with others.

Write your manuscript in a sequence that is interesting, give it an interesting title, and create an outstanding cover that makes the reader want to start reading.

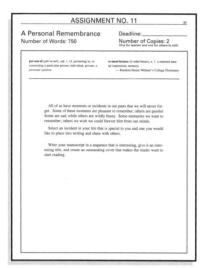

Printed on Page 89

*This assignment offers another big plus — It moves your students out of the safety of their classroom.*

Printed on Page 91

# ASSIGNMENT NO. 11 — A PERSONAL REMEMBRANCE

As you can see and as your students are bound to notice, you still are interested in them personally. Tell them you will welcome a remembrance they would like to share with you and the class. This assignment can bring an emotional potpourri for the whole class to savor and enjoy.

**Now give each student a copy of:**
**ASSIGNMENT SHEET NO. 11 — A PERSONAL REMEMBRANCE.**
**Read the Assignment Sheet aloud and explain the information.**

Be sure you give your students the date of the deadline, and have them write it on their copies.

**After you have finished reading, tell them:**
*CONQUER THE POWER OF THE WHITE!*
Start writing!

You know the procedure. Let them start writing. After a few minutes, walk around the room and give them instant approval.

They write their manuscripts. The manuscripts are edited, with corrections and constructive suggestions given.

After the manuscripts are corrected and refined, you will want to see the works. Then either you store the manuscripts or have your students retain a copy of their manuscripts in their notebooks.

Now you are ready to present the next and final assignment.

# ASSIGNMENT NO. 12 — A PROFILE OF A CREATIVE PERSON

**Give each student a copy of:**
**ASSIGNMENT SHEET NO. 12. — A PROFILE OF A CREATIVE PERSON.**
**Read the Assignment Sheet aloud and explain the information.**

Be sure you give your students the date of the deadline, and have them write it on their copies.

This is the longest and the most complex assignment of the course. It is in fact advisable that you allow more time for the completion of this paper, because of the required interviews the writers must hold and the necessary amout of research and organization they must do before composing the article.

No doubt — this piece is the *tour de force*. It is by far the most demanding. But by now, your writers should be ready for it. They have been researching, writing, editing, and rewriting for at least eleven weeks. Like athletes preparing for an Olympic competition, your students have stretched and strengthened their literary muscles in preparation for the big event and the ultimate challenge. This is it!

This assignment offers another big plus — It moves your students out of the safety of their classroom and forces each one of them to meet and tell about another person. Your students might approach the person who is to be interviewed by saying:

"I am a writer who is preparing to write an important profile about an accomplished creative person, and you are that person."

# A Profile of a Creative Person
Number of Words: 1,500

Deadline:_____

**Number of Copies: 2**
(One for teacher and one for others to edit)

---

**cre·a·tive** (krē-ā′tǐv), *adj.* 1. having the quality or power of creating. 2. resulting from originality of thought; imaginative.

**pro·file** (prō′fīl′), *n.* 7. an informal biographical sketch.
— Random House Webster's College Dictionary

---

Within our communities and neighborhoods, there are some very creative people. Not all creative people are painters or writers. Some are architects, cabinet makers, quilters, bakers, interior decorators, gardeners, and the like, who take special pride in the things they create.

In preparing to write A Profile of a Creative Person, do the following:

1. Select the person;
2. Interview that person;
3. Look carefully at the things he or she creates;
4. Interview at least two people who know the creative person.

In your profile, tell about the person. Describe the person physically. Tell how the person moves and speaks, and how he or she works. Include what motivates this person. Describe the things he or she creates. You may quote statements from the person and tell of that person's personal philosophy and professional goals.

You also may quote the other people you have interviewed and offer opinions of your own. If you wish, you may take photographs and include them in the profile, and/or make drawings or paintings to accompany your written profile.

Write your manuscript in a sequence that is interesting, give it an interesting title, and create an outstanding cover that makes the reader want to start reading.

*By the time the manuscripts are edited, refined, and completed, this is likely to be the assignment of which your students will be the most proud.*

This assignment also provides another turn of the screw that increases the pressure. It forces your writers to think about the questions they need to ask while they are conducting interviews. They will need to make notes and/or they may wish to tape-record their interviews. If any of the sessions are to be taped, by law the writers must first get permission from the people they will be recording.

In all probability, the people they interview will want to preview a copy of the manuscript before you hand it in, so the writer should allow time for this. Getting the subject's approval and blessing can add more pressure. Great! It lets the writers know that their manuscripts must be thoroughly prepared and well written. Editors will have more questions about punctuation and grammar. Paragraphing will be of the utmost importance, and the use of quotation marks will need to be checked. As your students are preparing this assignment, there probably will be more talking in class about the problems they are encountering.

The writers may say:

"My creative person doesn't talk much. He just says yes or no to my questions."

"Mine talks so much, I can't get all of my questions asked."

"My creative person is so interesting, I forget to ask questions."

By the time the manuscripts are edited, refined, and completed, this is likely to be the one piece of writing for which your students have done the most work and over which they have lost the most sleep. It also is likely to be the assignment of which they will be the most proud.

**After your students have conducted their interviews, they are ready to start, so tell them:**

*CONQUER THE POWER OF THE WHITE!*

Start writing!

You know the procedure. Your students know the procedure. They now are professional writers. They write their manuscripts. After the manuscripts are edited, corrected, refined, and completed, store them for safekeeping.

## Mission Accomplished!

You have done it!

Your students have now become literary producers!

If you have twenty student writers in your publishing company, they have enriched the world by producing 20 writers x 12 original manuscripts, which equals 240 pieces of writing.

More important than that: Each of those 240 pieces of writing has been carefully read, enjoyed, and edited by five editors — four other students, and you.

Even more important:

Your student writers have become literary thinkers!

CONGRATULATIONS!

Now it is time to assemble your writers' stories and articles and select the best ones for publication.

# It's Time To Go Public!

## Selecting the Best Works for Publication

You, the president of your publishing company, and your writers and your editors have some important decisions to make. At the beginning of the course, you told your writers that when all the assignments were completed, the best manuscripts would be selected and bound into a book. That book would then be presented to the school library so other students and teachers could read these outstanding pieces of writing, not only during the present school year, but for years to come.

Believe it or not, I am willing to leave the process by which you make those selections in the hands and minds of you and your students. However, I do have some thoughts and suggestions that you might wish to consider.

I hope every student writer has at least one piece of writing in the book, more if possible. This can easily be accomplished by having each writer select one, two, or three manuscripts of his or her own best work. And those one, two, or three pieces might automatically be included in the book.

Then, I think each editor might be allowed to nominate one outstanding manuscript from each assignment that was created by another student.

Next, have all the editors determine which outstanding examples constitute the best of each of the assignments. If you wish, have them select one, two, or three of them. They may select more examples, but if they do, you are going to wind up with a very thick book.

If you have a personal or professional favorite piece of writing that wasn't chosen by the writers or the editors, invoke your executive privilege as president of the publishing company and insist that the work be included!

I suggest having a special section added to the book that features brief biographies about your writers. That's one more writing assignment for the students, but it is one for which they are now well prepared to compose, and it is one they will thoroughly enjoy writing.

Have your students write their biographies, full of hype and good public relations adjectives. Forget all modesty. Go for broke!

*Have your students write brief biographies, full of hype and good public relations adjectives. Forget all modesty. Go for broke!*

## Should Your Publishing Company Publish One Book Or Two Books?

You and your editors have another choice to make:

Should you publish one book or two books?

The first book is the one composed of the articles and stories your writers have created. We have discussed that one.

However, it occurs to me that because of the assignment — A PROFILE OF A CREATIVE PERSON — you have something truly extraordinary to share with your school and community. If you have twenty writers, then you have twenty profiles of creative persons in your community. Now you have the opportunity to recognize the goals and achievements of these people by publishing a second book that includes all of their profiles.

Plus, both books would be very attractive, because they also will include the covers created for each article or story. And yes! If they choose to do so, your writers may improve any of their articles, stories, or covers before final publication.

There are easy and inexpensive ways to print the pages. You can photocopy them. That makes the weight and whiteness of all the sheets consistent. Also, when photocopying, you have the opportunity to print on both sides of the sheets.

If your school doesn't have a super-duper, state-of-the-art photocopier that you can use, a parent of one of your students might agree to make the use of one available to you at his or her office or home.

If that is not possible, talk to the owner or manager of a local shop where copies are made. Tell him or her what your class has done. Chances are, you will be allowed to make copies at a special rate, or perhaps free. That can provide good quality copies for you and good public relations for the shop.

There are several ways to bind the books — plastic comb or three-hole punch are the least expensive. But if you want something of better quality, and you don't have a book bindery in your community, go to a large city and find a bindery. Or explain your needs to a printer. The printer may be able to guide you to a place that can bind your book.

How good should the binding be? The very best and the very finest you can afford. If you can afford embossed gold lettering or a leather cover — go for it! If the best you can obtain is a plastic comb binding, with a hand-painted, handprinted cover — take that! Either way, your students are going to be proud of their achievements, because they know their writing is going to be included in a published book and placed in their school library for years to come.

## Time To Celebrate!

Create an event! Make it the most elegant event you can arrange, with an awards ceremony where each student writer is presented a *Certificate of Excellence* to honor his or her outstanding achievements in literature. A simple, but elegant proclamation, framed or suitable for framing, would be appropriate.

Be sure to invite the parents, family members, and friends of the writers. Also invite your school's principal, and the teachers, librarians, board of

*Your students are going to be proud of their achievements because they know their writing is going to be included in a published book and placed in their school library for years to come.*

education members, and the superintendent of the school district. Invite the mayor, too, and even the governor of your state if you are so inclined. And don't forget the merchants in your community who have helped you.

Make certain you invite the news media — television and newspapers — to report the event. Also be sure to have someone take pictures. After prints are made, you may want to add some of them to the books you have presented to the library.

By all means, invite the creative people who are featured in the profiles. You may even want to have the writers present these people with a complimentary copy of a book that includes his or her profile. If you cannot afford to present an entire book to each person, then have your students prepare individual booklets, including attractive covers for them, that hold only the respective subject's profile.

Yours is a literary event, not a soccer game. So no blue jeans or tennis shoes are allowed. You want all the writers dressed to the nines. The young men should be wearing white shirts, ties, and suits or sport jackets and slacks, along with dress shoes. Young ladies should wear dresses, or dressy skirts and blouses or sweaters, and appropriate shoes, of course.

For refreshments, high tea and crumpets would be fine. Or serve punch and hors d'oeurves, or punch and really special cookies.

Make sure that during the ceremonies, all speeches and presentations are kept short and to the point.

Having a short selection of music played on a piano, violin, or cello, alone or together, would enhance the atmosphere. The music should be classical, of course.

You want the ceremony to be an event which you, your writers, your editors, and your guests will never forget.

Finally, either you or one of your students should make the grand presentation to the library of the book or books you have published. The book or books may be presented to:

- The school librarian;
- The school principal;
- The superintendent of the school district; or
- Anyone else you and your writers feel would add some prestige to the occasion.

## This Is Not the End, It Is Really the Beginning

The book publication of your students' works and the celebration of their extraordinary achievements will bring a closure to the writing course. But those acts will not bring an ending. They will represent a beginning.

The improvements your students have made in their writing skills will continue. What your students have learned in your class will travel with them wherever they go. And their memory of you will go with them, too.

When I was a teenager, the first man for whom I worked taught me how to dice onions. Since then I have diced hundreds, maybe thousands, of them. I am one of the best onion-dicers you ever will meet. Every time I dice onions, I remember that man, and I recall how he took the time to teach

*Yours is a literary event, not a soccer game.*

*So no blue jeans or tennis shoes are allowed.*

*The music should be classical, of course.*

me that very useful skill.

A few years later, I had another employer who showed me how to place a ruler at a diagonal between two parallel lines and immediately be able to divide the distance between the lines into thirds, or fifths, or sevenths, or elevenths, or thirty-ninths, or any odd number that is usually difficult to compute without a calculator. As a graphics designer, I have used that skill hundreds, maybe thousands, of times. Every time I use it, I think of the man who took the time to teach me that very useful skill.

When I was in high school, I had a teacher who taught me how to write and edit stories and articles. Over the years, I have enjoyed writing and editing hundreds of stories and articles. Every time I write or edit, I think of the woman who took the time to teach me those important skills. Those skills have enabled me to write books and articles, and they prepared me to make a living in a very challenging and most pleasurable way.

Your students' improved writing and thinking skills will go with them to their homes, to college, to work, and to anywhere else they may go. Those skills will be with them whenever and wherever they may choose to utilize them. And when they use them, they will think of the wonderful man or woman who took the time to help them improve their writing skills and their thinking skills. They will remember you and realize that it was their privilege and good fortune to have had you as a teacher.

You will remember your students, too. You will recall their frustrations, their fears, their excitement, and their improvements. You will remember their stories — the real ones and the imaginary ones. You also will remember the stumbling blocks, the creative breakthroughs, and the earthshaking miracles. You'll remember the nonwriters who became first-time writers, the mediocre writers who became superb writers, and those strange and wonderful kids who astounded everyone with their off-the-wall approaches. You will remember who wrote prose that was so brilliant, it transcended into poetry. And you'll recall those students whom you wish you could have moved up just one more level.

Well, enough of that. It will soon be time for you to start thinking about next year's crop. Your new students probably will be a mixed bag. They usually are. But whatever they are, they'll all have two brains — a left one and a right one, an academic one and a creative one.

Your job will be to get these students to use both of their brains in order to improve their writing and thinking skills. Then they, too, will be able to write outstanding stories and articles that will inform, excite, entertain, and inspire their readers.

By now — you certainly know how to do that!

*Your students' improved writing and thinking skills will go with them to their homes, to college, to work, and to anywhere else they may go.*

*Those skills will be with them whenever and wherever they may choose to utilize them.*